Confusion? Or Apathy!

Evolution of Man Starts Today

"RAM, ROM, Hard and Soft Disc
Drives of the Human Brain."

Copyrighted in 1975 and stolen out of the Copyright Office.
Copyrighted in 1979 and stolen out of the Copyright Office.
Copyrighted in 1981 and is still in the Copyright Office they no longer allow visitors to the document room. They remembered Registering and storing my Registrations. I made Physiology discoveries as to the physics of the working brain and added it and anatomy references to this book and Copyrighted the changes in 1987. Published by Thampson Shore Books 1988 and distributed to all Graduate Universities in the U.S. and some abroad. I thought if they all new who wrote it they would not plagiarize me. I was wrong. This is technical facts. Even though I discovered these facts -- they can be repeated. But my name has not been quoted (knowing I have been having a hard time and they did not review my work) Not very nice of them is it. They were probably afraid. I do not blame them. Although I had amnesia that people were threatening me. A 'heads up' would have been nice.

Added an addendum to this book Copyrighted in 1998 with my 1994 discovery that Lack of Noradrenalin in parts of the brain causes dreaming or voices when awake. May also be caused by to much Serotonin in parts of the Brain.

Prologue: Everyone suffers from at leased a slight amount of Mental illness -- which I call psychological illness. To avoid painful thoughts and memories which would cause physical illness. We take on falls roles and mimic. In other words we loose our minds and do and think what the role we are or who we are mimicking, would do or think. By not having our own thoughts we avoid any conflict. We may be having many conflicts but as long as we do not have to acknowledge these conflicts they do not affect us. But the walking dead could be a good description of one of these people. A good example is when we hate something about a parent or friend and start behaving the same way. This is not genetics this is avoidance. And denial, and issues on the back burner. We have a lot of useful euphemisms like this, But we are in such denial we do not realize what we are saying. Such as the decision of Psychiatrists to call Lack of Noradrenaline in parts of the brain Schizophrenia actually I am Greek so I know the word itself means what I am now talking about. When someone behaves like someone ells or a split personality which we all have been subject to. Learning is mimicry and it is built into our system. It also has a logical basis or programmed basis. It can always be traced to its rudiments the fear of death; Disguised as Home sickness, fear of aging, fear of germs, even fear of loosing ones job. The uncertainty! The paradox! How can you love everything in life if dying is part of life. Paradox is also a form for computer viruses and the brain is a computer and it is subject to these viruses of a programming nature based on the way God comes up with these Ideas through random nature dumb being the operative word to create things to be in paradise God gets his Ideas from Random Nature so we must take the bad mistakes of creation with the Good Mistakes of creation for the time being. Believe in Paradise but do not kill your self we Have people who love us even strangers and we have responsibilities to build a foundation of beauty and goodness that will fallow us into heaven. Some one said something to Carl Marx like this and he had a nervous brake down and blamed religion imagining if he had no knowledge of this wishful thinking he would have been content. Not so! If you brake your arm

p2

in my case a finger twice then you feel less pain the second time. This is because pain is confusion in the Brain. And death is a paradox and it will always be painful. Unless you have faith. This Book is the Science of the brain and thought. I invented the term Neurophysicist because I had no degree and it was difficult to explain to people what I did. I also invented the term Independent Psychological Researcher. At the age of Three I noticed how people plaid roles to avoid painful thoughts, I was taught at church that Jesus told his disciples to prophesize and that He said "I wish all men could be saved" I noticed how adults were kind of hypocritical. If Jesus wishes something obvious, to me it means it will come true -- so I decided God was telling me to cure Mental (as in thought) Illness. I boasted of my faith, and my parish priest confided in me that he was not sure there was a God. I said It is obvious there is a God he is all around us and he speaks to me through the events in the day and how my life would tern out over the years.

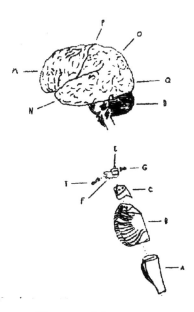

Chapter 1 important terms & Processes:

Hard Disc Drive- is the permanent storage of memories as we sleep Memories are pulses of energy traveling through our nerves the number of pulses increases throughout the day till the nerves are purged of these signals these memories are then placed in another storage system chemical or other unknown form of memory storage. Because there are more signals in the nervous system later in the day the clock is perceived as moving slower and moving faster in the morning because each pulse of energy is relative time ticking away the more thoughts the more time elapses ware as the mechanical clock remains constant.

ROM Language—Mechanical design for sequential memory storage: retrieval and memory cross-referencing, Sequential timing Equation (mechanical design of thought); and the divine wish to make use of this mechanism (to exist); Therefore the wish to love everything in life, because if you do not love everything in life you cannot be completely happy (and presently no one is).

ROM Language paradox- you can not enjoy everything such as death if death means you would not be able to enjoy anything.

ROM Memory- see Hard Disc Drive.

RAM Language- the formation of schizophrenic role-playing to avoid paradoxes.

RAM Memory- Both the mechanical storage of memory in the nervous system based on biochemical conductance circuitry and Hard Disc Memory.

Software- see RAM Memory.

Thalamus- Four of the five main senses pass through the thalamus, then branch out to the Cerebral Hemispheres. The thalamus is a sequential transistor switching device, separating the brains function into four main topics: Eye sight, Hearing, Glandular Secretions of the Pituitary Gland, and involuntary (smooth) muscle operation. The Thalamus also controls sleep cycles; it paralyzes voluntary muscles during dream sleep except for the partial voluntary diaphragm muscle controlling breathing.

Cerebellum- Most active of the Cerebral Hemispheres. First to be activated in thought formation. One of its functions is to control the voluntary muscles in cooperation with the rest of the brain. The Motor Area of the Frontal Lobe gives out instructions to voluntary muscles. The Cerebellum monitors what is actually occurring in order to guide and correct the movements. (From memory)

Hypothalamus- like the Thalamus it divides the functions of the brain, the Hypothalamus deals mainly with Homeostasis of body chemistry and organ functions; Such as: temperature, hunger, thirst, sexual activity and endocrine functions. The Hypothalamus affects sequential timing of the sense of smell. Smell is the only sense to bypass the Thalamus; For this reason the sense of smell functions while you are asleep, and is absent from dream sleep dreams. The Hypothalamus acts as a biological clock for goal setting of he mind.

Pineal Gland- Literally a clock. It has light sensitive cells which react to light which passes through our skulls probably from the eyes, ears, and sinuses. The entire brain uses the Pineal Gland Clock to tell the time of day; Mainly through connections to the Hypothalamus.

Nuclear Raphe Cells- Neurons in the Brain Stem, that use blood cells as neuronal sensors in ascertaining metabolic changes in the body. If blood passing through the Medulla Oblongata is oxygen poor respiration increases.

Astrocytes- Neurons in the CNS which have contact with veins. One of their functions is to use the blood supply to collect a negative electric charge that is released into the extra cellular fluid CSF around the cerebral brain and Axons of the spinal cord. Some Astrocytes act as grounds for other cells, and control maximum charge in the Cerebrospinal Fluid. Blood collects its Electric Charge from Friction. (Discovered by this author). *p. 6*

Neurons- Message initiating brain or nerve cells.

Oligodendrocytes- Neurons, which affect the signals of, true Brain Neurons (CNS Neurons), their function is unknown. They make Astrocyte and Schwann Cell type attachments.

Schwann Cell- see chap.III

Frontal Lobe- Coordinates thought the way the Cerebellum coordinates movement. The lower area of the Frontal lobe (commonly more on the left side of the brain) is concerned with actual speech and thought, defined in word form. The area of the Frontal Lobe bordering the Central Sulcus is involved with voluntary muscle coordination (called the Motor Area) damage to this area on one side of the brain can cause paralysis of the opposite half of the body.

Temporal Lobe- information from the hearing senses are accepted at the top area of the Temporal Lobe.

Parietal Lobe- There is no visual boundary between the Parietal, Occipital and Temporal Lobes. The Parietal Lobe is involved with: Reading, the Taste sense, Sensory messages of heat, touch, and pain, enter the Parietal Lobe along the border of the Central Sulcus.

Central Sulcus- A fold cited as a point of reference. See sketch

Microglia- smallest of the brain cells. Have the same cleanup responsibilities as a white blood cell.

Occipital Lobe- identifies visual images; recalls visual images, and determines the point of interest in visual scanning.

Pseudounipolar Neuron- are located in Spinal Ganglions, and Pons; they are connected to Axons bringing messages from Sensory Neurons. They allow the sensory messages to pass; at the same time they are recording those messages and in delayed time release the same messages in a form that can be recognized as a memory; completing the RAM Memory cycle. The Brain recognizes the type of memory by its route of origin.

Chapter II a matter of timing

There are millions of processes going on in the body at the same time and the brain controls every one of them. Yet we are not consciously aware of many of these processes. We often can concentrate on something so hard that we are not listening to our surroundings, yet when someone calls us by name, we hear it or we do not hear anything yet we turn around to see who is calling. The reason we heard our name when it seemed like we heard nothing else, is because we always hear everything around us but we do not always remember what we heard, because if we gave less thought to something we heard, there is less to remember. It is not that we do not remember our quicker thoughts, but usually we remember them at the same quick speed, even though we would be trying to analyze the memory at a slower speed.

Every process of the body is controlled by it's (your) single mind. We move and think just as the two-dimensional pictures (frames) of a movie appear to move and have three dimensions. Each part of the brain and spinal cord (the spinal cord is part of the brain) divides the sensory signals and memory components. Into sequential units in time (they take specific turns). Each memory sequence moves cyclically through the nervous system, and is added upon as long as the subject stays awake.

A simplified description of a Neuron would be to call it a Variable Oscillation Capacitor, and self regulating signal separation switch and junction.

Memory is a continually flowing pattern of signals, each topic being placed within a specific time frame and sequential order. Each signal for one topic is identical to the signals of other topics, only the position that the signal holds in reference to the other signals is different. Each signal enters the Cerebral Lobes in a different spot creating the differences in each memory.

While you sleep signals in the nervous system are transferred to the Hard Disc. This leaves your nervous system holding fewer memories fewer pulses of electricity, leaving more spaces. In the space of time when these blanks occur the brain is left inoperative, There fore time moves more quickly in the morning. Physical exhaustion can also cause memories to be transferred to the Hard Disk; this causes clocks from your point of view to speed up.

CHAPTER III
Chemistry of signal transport through Axons discovered by Arthur P. Vavoudis

Brain signals are transported by way of axons each Neuron releases a chemical Neuro Transmitter The reaction of which creates heat forcing potassium (P) out of the axon through spaces between molecules making up the axon wall. Excited potassium passing into the extracellular fluid (CSF) excites chlorine (CL) atoms, and forces small stable sodium (Na) atoms into the axon, as this occurs: (NaCl) Sodium Chloride Electrolyte is formed, which allows the ever present electric charge in the Cerebrospinal fluid to travel through the axon. A partial vacuum in the axon after the potassium's departure, coincides with the opening of Receptor Molecules, stimulated by the entering electric charge which in turn allows the original K-Cl-Na Soup to enter the axon forcing out the sodium (Na) and stopping the reaction.

The use of Schwann cells (electrical capacitors) in the PNS, as negatively charged Potassium leaves the axon in the vicinity of a Schwann Cell, the Schwann Cell contracts squeezing its contents (negatively charged Sodium Atoms) into the axon. Potassium is pulled back into the axon at the Node of Ranvier as the Schwann Cell vacuums back into itself (on recoil) the now neutrally uncharged Sodium Atoms from the axon, the reaction is stopped.

CHAPTER IV Learning mechanism and the one true paradox

The Brain is a computer which assembles our thoughts but thoughts do not come from the brain, they come entirely from the environment and always pertain to the continuation of life which is our memory combined with the wish to live and love everything in life, and continued memorization of same.

It is possible to build a machine that can learn. A mobile device can have a pattern of motion programmed into it. When this device bumps into something, that turn in its programming is changed at random. Then it reverses back to where it began and then starts over this time avoiding the obstruction.

There is no such thing as luck. When some one tosses a coin, what side that coin falls on, depends on how hard the coin is thrown, and what kind of spin it is given, these are things our subconscious has to calculate in order to toss a coin in the first place. Meaning whether you win or lose depends on whether your subconscious lets the other guy win. There is a logical reason for everything even if there is not a proven reason.

In order for something to exist, there must be an explanation of how it came to exist and in order for there to be an explanation of each explanation in succession, the explanation must go on for infinity. Since each explanation for the existence of something is infinite (never ending) then there can be no explanation for the existence of anything. The previous statement, by itself, is illogical unless we assume that a God is constantly creating our existence, distant past, and future.

The psychology in this book is based on the knowledge that our basic biological programming (ROM Language) and that of all living things, is the wish to live and love everything in life, death having no part in our ROM Language. Even though knowledge is infinite and we will go on learning forever, our comprehension is limited, because God creates all that we know and will know.

CHAPTER V Instinct defined

Instinct is made up of two things, Physical ability, and the ROM Language. Instincts believed to be biologically inherited are actually learned knowledge or schizophrenic behavior. Such as the fear of heights in infants, Up to the age of eight months an infant has no fear of heights (see chap. VII) after the age of eight months the infant develops a sense of self, and of its parents concerns, along with it a fear of heights.

If a researcher truly observes a chicken hatch from an egg. With food all around it, the first thing it does is smell the food, it then lowers its head to see the food, and to smell it better, then the chick strikes it with its beak to see what it feels like, this breaks the kernel causing it to give off more scent, the chicken then picks it up in its mouth, picking its aroma up in its mouth, then feels it and tastes it with its tongue, then almost automatically swallows it. There was no instinct other than the wish to live and love everything in life including its own senses, which enabled the chicken to teach itself how to eat without any specific instructions.

The migration of monarch butterflies is explained by the monarchs ultraviolet eye sight water does not give off ultraviolet light so the monarch avoids bodies of water they follow the sun as it travels South and stop I Mexico right ware the climate changes to a tropical night temperature.

p. 10

Pointing by dogs is a non-instinct. If you look at a slow motion film of a Pointer running you will see how its pointing stance is the position its limbs take while in quick stride. An untrained dog starts out chasing animals then learns that he can get closer to the other animal by creeping up on it and by freezing in sprinting stance when the target gets nervous or looks up.

Even the predatory instinct is not. If a predator is taken from its parent right at birth and fed nothing that tastes like meat without a role model, that predator would never intentionally kill, even when released into the wild. Animals have died in such cases.

The one ROM Language combined with physical ability (aptitude) when closely analyzed accounts for all of the behavioral differences between different species of animals.

It has been proven that the migratory routes of birds are learned and not instinctive and that their navigation abilities are due to Compass Cells. Each Compass Cell has a peace of Magnetite in it, which moves toward the northern wall of the cell. These cells have also been found in human beings, but this sense is not usually developed due to our reliance on our intelligence to navigate by symbolic landmarks.

I have observed during the hawk migration how young birds follow their parents on the hawk migration routs.

Wildebeest migrate in large circles for exercise, and food picking excellence learned behavior forgotten no longer natural to the American Bison.

I believe even the brain of a honey bee is complex enough to teach themselves a dance language as to where to find honey.

CHAPTER VI

The brain does have a bearing on the type of intelligence for different species, and the mentally retarded. Other species of animals have a greater Brain Stem capacity in comparison to the Cerebral Hemisphere.
The Cerebral Hemisphere- divides thought into topical sequences. The Brain Stem- divides the senses into separate timing sequences, making animals more conscious of their surroundings, shortening their attention span. The Mentally Retarded have less brain cells to do the same amount of work, the brain can do a

great deal of rerouting of messages to healthy Neurons, increasing the number of messages each cell must relay. It is not the quantity of knowledge but the speed in which various topics are absorbed, which is retarded, ROM memory is not affected. Since mentally retarded Human Beings have the same attention span as other people they become discouraged limiting the number of steps in a single concept.

Chapter VII A matter of timing continued

The recall of memories is triggered by our senses. All stimulus and thought symbolize past experiences, triggering the systematic recollection of memories until the correct memory is found. More current, significant, and longer memories are recalled first. Recall is used to terminate one subject of thought so that the individual can move on to another.

A Biological Clock plays a very significant role in determining our attention span. When we preoccupy ourselves during a certain time of day, during the same time the next day, that thought or activity will be recalled, each time we repeat a pattern of thought or behavior the memory of this activity becomes stronger the next day, at the same time of day.

The Pineal Gland (Biological Clock) plays a major role in goal seeking and habit, but every Neuron works as a separate timing mechanism.

The principle of memory by association is the linking of what is to be memorized with a more prominent memory, which receives more attention from our biological clockwork brain.

The rest of this glossary is devoted to the names of the different areas of the brain and at least one of their functions, which I learned from numerous sources including the coloring book of the brain. New and old energy tracing equipment has shown that the entire brain is involved in memory retrieval and thought formation. The: Frontal, Parietal, Occipital, Temporal and Cerebellum have partially autonomous functions.

Medulla Oblongata- two of its functions are heart rate, and respiratory timing.

Pons- Correlation of signals between the cerebellum,, Midbrain, and the Cerebral Lobes is one of the functions of the Pons.

Midbrain- What the Pons is to the limbs, the Midbrain is to the visual and auditory muscles.

KEY TO FIGURES

(A) MEDULLA OBLONGATA

(B) PONS

(C) MIDBRAIN

(D) CEREBELLUM

(E) THALAMUS

(F) HYPOTHALAMUS

(G) PINEAL GLAND

(H) ASTROCYTE

(I) NEURONS

(J) OLIGODENDROCYTES:
  1. SATELLITE
  2. INTERFASCIC
  3. AND VASCULAR

(K) SCHWANN CELLS

(L) AXON

(M) FRONTAL LOBE

(N) TEMPORAL LOBE

(O) PARIETAL LOBE

(P) CENTRAL SULCUS

(Q) OCCIPITAL LOBE

(R) MICROGLIA

(S) PSEUDOUNIPOLAR
    NEURON

(T) PITUITARY GLAND

(U) SPINAL CORD

p. 13

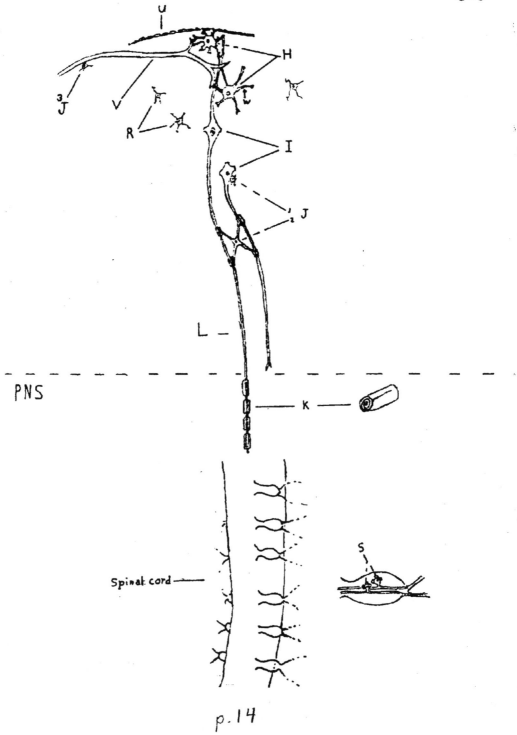

PNS

Spinal cord

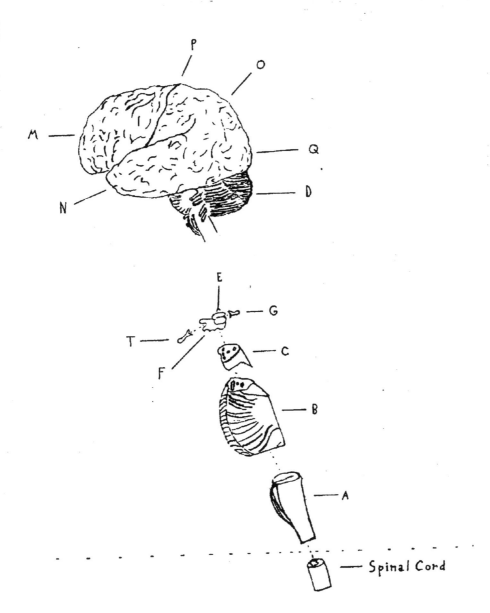

P

O

M

Q

N

D

E

G

T

F

C

B

A

Spinal Cord

p. 15

Behavior is controlled in the same way as thought. Often a person will be thinking about one subject while performing an unrelated task. These actions are patterned after the previous day. The longer these actions are repeated the stronger the pattern becomes, because the memory of this activity becomes greater. In order to break habits the pattern must be broken resetting the biological clock.

For students to better learn at school each subject must be held at the same time of day each day.

Chapter VIII Development of RAM and ROM reasoning

The conscious brain waves up to age two become the subconscious brain waves. At the age of one the child realizes he can make other people happy this is distorted into the RAM Language "the wish to be loved by everyone" which is distorted into the wish to be made happy by everyone. All thought is developed upon the ROM, and RAM Languages. When the brain has a conflicting problem between ROM "the wish to love everything" and RAM "the wish to make others love you" it causes depression, which is the increasing fixation on an unsolvable problem, The only solutions being, to change or disavow the RAM Language, or to temporarily replace that problem with unrelated thoughts, but the abandoned problem will then reoccur periodically and will continue to reoccur until the RAM Language is disavowed or changed.

Unlike ROM Language, which is permanent, RAM Language can be disavowed or altered.
It is important that the memory that the RAM L. has been changed reoccurs along with the memory of the old RAM Language.

Chapter IX What am I?

The body you had when you were 3 years old 'was not the body you had when you were 5 years old' the body you had at the age of 12 was not the body you had at age 5 either. If you are over 21 no part of the body you have today existed when you where 12, except your teeth. You are continually flushing your body down the drain and what you 'consume' becomes your new body. What you flushed down the toilet eventually becomes part of someone else's body.   We all

p. 16

Behavior is controlled in the same way as thought. Often a person will be thinking about one subject while performing an unrelated task. These actions are patterned after the previous day. The longer these actions are repeated the stronger the pattern becomes, because the memory of this activity becomes greater. In order to break habits the pattern must be broken resetting the biological clock.

For students to better learn at school each subject must be held at the same time of day each day.

Chapter VIII Development of RAM and ROM reasoning

The conscious brain waves up to age two become the subconscious brain waves. At the age of one the child realizes he can make other people happy this is distorted into the RAM Language "the wish to be loved by everyone" which is distorted into the wish to be made happy by everyone. All thought is developed upon the ROM, and RAM Languages. When the brain has a conflicting problem between ROM "the wish to love everything" and RAM "the wish to make others love you" it causes depression, which is the increasing fixation on an unsolvable problem, The only solutions being, to change or disavow the RAM Language, or to temporarily replace that problem with unrelated thoughts, but the abandoned problem will then reoccur periodically and will continue to reoccur until the RAM Language is disavowed or changed.

Unlike ROM Language, which is permanent, RAM Language can be disavowed or altered.
It is important that the memory that the RAM L. has been changed reoccurs along with the memory of the old RAM Language.

Chapter IX What am I?

The body you had when you were 3 years old was not the body you had when you were 5 years old, the body you had at the age of 12 was not the body you had at age 5 either. If you are over 21 no part of the body you have today existed when you where 12, except your teeth. You are continually flushing you body down the drain and what you consume becomes your new body. What you flushed down the toilet eventually becomes part of someone else's body. We all share the same body in that respect. We are all creations of God's imagination, in both ways we are God, one being. But we are not one being we are separate distinct beings. If we are individual beings but as explained not a single body, if we are not a body then what are we. What is it that is distinctly different about one living thing compared to another: Only two things, our Blueprints (DNA) and our Memory.

Anyone under hypnosis, given a name the person's address and a time and date, the person can experience the memory of the named person even when that person is still alive, showing that similar experiences by people have been misconstrued to be reincarnation.

CHAPTER X
GENETIC DIFFERENCES IN MAN

The reason each human being looks different from every other human being, is the same reason each chimpanzee looks different from every other chimpanzee: it is no each member of a community (pride) can be recognized from a distance. This effect is quite intentional and no matter how inbred men become the offspring would look different from the parents.

Identical twins do look exactly alike because they have the same genes with the exception of one gene mutation which gives the egg two brain wave patterns (tuned frequency of memory signals) instead of one. The nucleus of the egg transposes instructions from the genes into Hard Disc Signals, which become the timing mechanism (ROM L. Computer Program) which controls embryo development. In the mutation being discussed two separate blueprints are created (the duplication of functions) causing the egg to divide into two embryos; Although this trait is called a mutation it is fairly common and successful evolution wise.

Internal organs of the body do not vary much from person to person since each human being's physical needs are the same. Only a die'off of all the people with a specific genetic trait can cause such an evolutional change to take place. Such as in primitive times: when people with wide eyes, living on glaciers died after becoming snow blind. When people with less pigment in there skin died at an earlier age from radiation exposure. When people with more pigment were politically isolated from the Northern Hemisphere. And in times when selective infanticide was practiced, to avoid razing a retarded child; by killing any infant that did not resemble the parent, or conceptual idea of attractiveness.

p. 18

There is no discernable difference between the brain of someone of one race and another brain of any other race; This was learned through the slicing and mapping of thousands of cadaver brains.

Most of the perceived differences between races are illusionary; such illusions start out as political propaganda name-calling. The people who first make these racial slurs do not really believe what they say; they have an ulterior motive. But then people will remember the slur so that they tend to notice any one of that race begaving like the stereotype; then do not notice when they (or the same person) does not behave like the stereotype. It is like believing in a Jinx; you notice when things are going wrong in the vicinity of a person but not when things are going right. Apathy can make a stereotype come true when those who do not fit that description keep silent.

Chapter XI Sexual development

Your first feelings regarding sex are that of resentment toward the roles of modesty since you have none. Next at an early age during a moment in time when you have no close friend you fantasize about going steady or being married which meant having a friend that is always there with you; This comes usually before you know, or care to know where babies come from, about age 5. At the age of 6 children start to notice how older people are disturbed by nudity. By the age seven they have become self-conscious about their body. This involuntary imposition of modesty into their lives causes them to have fantasies in opposition to their sexual parts, or fantasies about a society where you do not need to wear clothes.

Sexual organs control mechanism begin developing at age 7 in girls, age 8 in boys, it takes two to three more years for the males to ejaculate, but were creating sperm as early as age 4. I heard women are less likely to miscarry after the age of 19.

Sexual development includes development of a signal system in the brain to turn the system on. The individual's sexual fantasies during puberty at age ten become the software for determining activation of the sexual organs. The typical scenario goes as follows: Your sexual parts seem to take on a life of their own. These new senses are not resented having not been completely unexpected. We try to mediate an understanding and acceptance of the new sense. This arouses our curiosity, and a number of questions arise; The question why is apparent, but what is it exactly and how does it work?, is not! Obviously if it is for making babies it involves the opposite sex and questions regarding their parts and function is much more of a mystery, so the sight of the opposite sex naked and even dressed peaks our curiosity becoming the dominant "On-Switch" for our sex related glands. Our earliest fantasies of having a relationship with a single individual of the opposite sex reoccur at this time.

When our thoughts recede supposedly form the topic of sex, we are still looking more closely at people of the opposite gender and they are looking more closely at us. This is when we become curious about our appearance and quite literally look at ourselves in a mirror for the first time and find ourselves staring at an unfamiliar pattern of light waves. Yet when we look at someone else's reflection or picture, we feel as though we are actually looking at the person because that is how we recognize people, by their image. But that is not the way we recognize ourselves (the same can be said for our voice). So when we look into a mirror we get the feeling that people can not see us for what we are. This leads to the delusion that we are not in control over our appearance and life as others see us. The truth is that people can see past our appearance just as we see past theirs. When we look at a friend we see a personality (memory), not a lifeless mannequin as we appear to ourselves.

My advice to adolescents is to see yourself as your healthy friends see you. Get used to, and love your own appearance. Develop good posture. When you love your own appearance it creates a confidence which can be seen by others and is attractive!

Chapter XII Language

Language and memory are one in the same thing we use language to compute ideas as well as to communicate.
As infants we learn the language of letter sounds and facial expressions, it is easy for a three-year-old to look at someone and tell what they are thinking. A more conscious adult understanding of early languages will help in lie detection methodology.

Baby language definitions Copyrighted in One Words One Lip of the Whole World © 1991 Mistakenly equated it with babble but it is older the earliest rudiments of language:

Definition	Hieroglyph

A= subject at a distance. Is an up side down vase with a negative sign in it for the water or energy flowing out of it from negative to positive ground.

B= Is for numbering.   Is a bearded wheat grain or and a double grave; small b is a fishing real casting out the reels always turn with the earth Clockwise.

C= Place in or place in this spot.   Is a cove or cattle booth, pen, or trap.

D= Road inward or Road.   Is a grave symbol. Small "d" is a fishing reel, reeling in.

E= food for the body or food for the mind. East spanning shadows or Fork. Small "e" is an ear and a mouth.

F= Up on in for.   Is a grain mill. Small "f" a staff.

G= Save seed, save the girl.   Is a germinating seed. Small "g" also a germinating seed.

H= "For"   Is a ladder. Small "h" is a chair.

I= good.   Depicts "Rain"

J= is for numbering water.   Depicts seeping ground water. Fish Hook.

K= place.   One is less than sign. The Right Hand of Christ.

L= left in that place.   Sun Dial. After Noon.

M= Face me.   Mountain. Gears of the Earth.

N= Is in.   Haven't the foggiest. Small "n" is a garden heap or kings grave.

O= positive nature; God makes it to rain when rain is needed.   A theta without a negative sign. A cover or well.

P= up in, bring in.   The real above a well.

Q= remember   a safety line as in spelunking.

R= Road out.   A "p" spilling water. Small "r" a branch.

S= return   A worm.

T= Sign   A crucifix.

U= See   A horseshoe.

V= for numbering food or water.   Is a Vase.

W= waves of water, light, gravity, and air.   Gears of the Sun.

X= x marcs the spot   Focus point.

Y= spilling, gratitude, skill.   Spilling honey.
Z= the path; paradise.   Path of a Bee.

Chapter XIII Night Dreams

Night-Dreams are the same creative thoughts that make up Day Dreams and except for the fact that messages arriving from our conscious senses are suppressed while we sleep. The Thalamus during dream sleep changes the route (path) of signals arriving and leaving from four of the five main senses, the sense of smell being the exception. Signals originating in the brain can then pass through the Thalamus, Mid Brain, and Pons; as if these signals were originating from sensory neurons. Giving the feeling that you are actually: Hearing, Seeing, Feeling temperature, and feeling touch. The difference between Night Dreams and reality our memory that the dream is a creation of our own imagination. Since instructions entering the Oculomotor Nerve bypass the Thalamus the eyes move during Night Dreams as if they were actually looking at what we are picturing in our dream.

How to relay conscious ideas to dream sleep subconscious; By making a self-hypnotic suggestion during meditation.
The following is the hypnotic suggestion I gave my self at age 8 in order to stop having nightmares and it worked. "A person has enough unhappy and frightening

experiences in life to learn to cope and survive under such conditions, without having to invent other such experiences in our imaginations, It only adds to what is wrong in the world. If one is to learn from dreams then they should be manipulated to have happy conclusions, for this reason I will never have another nightmare".

CHAPTER XIIII RAM Language based on ROM Language

HAPPINESS- is the opposite of unhappiness, which occurs when things do not occur the way we instinctively wish them to.

CURIOSITY- Our senses do nothing but gather information then when we think, we are taking this knowledge and rearranging it to form new ideas. Without the wish to understand, life stops. Curiosity: is ROM L. – the wish to love everything; the wish to live, in other words- to be happy. All living things have this instinct.

THE WISH TO BE LOVED BY EVERYONE- is not to be confused with ROM Language. "The wish to be loved by everyone" develops later from biological needs: The instinct to eat, to sleep, and to avoid pain...

LOVE- is the measure of importance anyone or thing has in your life.

LOVE AND SEX- The attraction between males and females is of RAM language origin. Seals and horses have harems; this insures that the most hardy proliferate since weaker males would not be able to attract mates and many more females are born than males. Many species who only breed once a year when conditions are favorable switch mates each year since there is only an attraction during the mating season, these species survive better on their own. Hawks seek out the same mate each year and migrate as family units.

   The family structure of man is closely related to the family structure of members of the parrot family. Parrots take life long mates because like man the ratio of males to females is close to equal. And the parrot has more free time, causing the parrot to demand more attention, spouses are chosen for their genetic health, the courtship rituals of which are stressful and cause insecurity, deterring monogamous species from seeking more than one bride. The birds that do not adopt the monogamous behavior die sooner due to communicable diseases and parasites, making learned behavior a matter of Natural Selection, in both wildlife and man.

p. 23

MORALITY- Any logic pertaining to ROM Language fulfillment.

MOOD- is how you feel over all. It is a scale of emotion, with any of an infinite number of combinations.

SENSE OF HUMOR- Depression is only a state of mind. We feel depressed when things are not going the way we instinctively know they should be. When we make fun of life we realize how good living makes us feel, and most important it makes light of unnecessary RAM Language Programming which we fall into, creating problems which do not actually exist, or magnify the problems that do. The realization of the unimportance of those problems brings a burst of emotion. The dropping of current problem fixations which are flooding (slowing) signal transmission in the nervous system, the resulting sudden increase of Signal Energy (rate of flow) causes laughter. Tickling causes too many neurons to fire causing spasms- laughter.

PRIDE- Is the good feelings you have when you emphasize your sense of purpose (reason based on ROM Language. False pride is based on RAM Language.

SENSE OF PURPOSE- is the explanation one gives oneself for wishing to love everything and the assumed reason for being alive. We can no more live without these rationalizations of what the purpose of our existence is, than we could live without memory. This is why having control of our own lives is so imperative and why lack of control causes role playing and personality changes in the outer consciousness.

CHAPTER XV Self hypnosis how to do it

  It is resting your brain to use subconscious parts of the brain without falling asleep
By making suggestions in this state you can impress goals onto the subconscious and the health of your body.

CHAPTER XVI DRUGS

  While we will create elaborate diversions of thought to masque (hide from) pain (pain- is confusion) the conscious mind will use drugs for the same reason. By speeding up or slowing down signals in the nerves system fixations on unresolved problems and confusion is avoided. Since the drug never resolves the conflict In

p. 24

the mind, and because the body will compensate for the drug, a chronic escalating psychological habit is formed, because the body begins to rely on the drug for chemical processes in the nervous system, a biological dependence is formed. GIFT TO YOUR TEACHER wording from "Cartoon Book of English Spelling" © 1995 by Arthur P. Vavoudis" was originally published in Evolution of Man Starts Today Copyright 1979 by Arthur P. Vavoudis' 1975 discovery:

I have something to say to the class today. Something we teachers were just taught, so that we can teach it to our students.

It is about Neuro Science, that is the study of how the brain works.

The brain is a device, which (among other processes) takes memories and makes thoughts out of them.

I was asked – Do you remember every face that you see in a day?

The answer I had was "No! I do not".

I am told that you have to stop and think about something before you can remember it, but in order to stop and think about something your brain has to be cued to stop what its thinking and think about something else!

How many of you know what the word cued means? – Let's see hands…

A cue can be the last word in a sentence that an actor playing a part in a play says before the next actor speaks and the next actor has memorized that word, so when the actor hears that word he knows it is his turn to speak.

Let's say someone is walking down a street with his best friend and a dog starts barking at him. His friend says all dogs bark at you! He says:

"No they do not!"

But because of the suggestion and because it was his best friend speaking – He releases a chemical in the brain called Dopamine. This chemical highlights the memory as one to remember – Like you use a highlighting pen in your book or on notes.

From then on do to the suggestion that all dogs bark at him he will only notice dogs that are barking at him. And when he thinks back he will not remember any dogs that were not barking at him.   p. 25

Can you tell me what he would be feeling or thinking? – That's right he would ether be afraid of dogs or he would begin hating dogs.

THAT IS WHAT PREJUDICE IS!

The subject of highlighting memories – making some memories stand out and be noticed more than other memories; brings us to the subject of drug addiction (that includes cigarettes and alcohol).

We make some memories more noticeable and at the same time the brain filters out other thoughts and signals while we remember the highlighted memories with the use of dopamine.

Other drugs act as a substitute for dopamine – and what are the memories that are highlighted when some one takes a drug? Do any of you know the answer?

Yes! It is the taking of the drug which is the memory that is highlighted and only taking the drug becomes important to someone taking drugs! And the more drugs some one takes – the memories that the person used to love become unimportant, and only taking the drug becomes important.

Notice how used to is spelled like "use" because you use memories to love life and to do anything you need to use your memory.

So we now know that addiction starts with the first puff on a cigarette. So do not try anything you could become addicted to. Get high on life. Do not become a slave to Drugs.

Chapter XVII Emotional Illness

Emotional illness is the result of emotional suffering. Everything, which affects us emotionally, can affect us physically. When we injure ourselves we feel pain which lets us know that something is wrong, yet when the pain stops, the message to the brain about what is wrong, is still being sent. Pain is not the message to the brain, it is the mental anguish (confusion) the message has caused, in the same way emotional stress would cause physical problems, if it were not for the ability to create an illusionary character, making it possible to hide from reality or emotional conflicts. *p. 26*

All thought is developed upon the ROM, and RAM Languages. When the brain has a conflict between R"OM (to love e everything in life), and RAM (to be made happy by others etcetera) it causes depression; which is the increasing fixation on an unsolvable problem (this slows down the brain). The only solutions being: to change or disregard the RAM Language, or to temporarily replace that problem with unrelated thoughts, but the abandoned problem will then reoccur periodically and will continue to reoccur until that RAM >language is disavowed (changed); this is called REOCCURRING DEPRESSION. Reoccurring Depression Cycles can be lengthened and the attacks of depression shortened, by dominance of the conscious mind by RAM Programming over ROM Language, this condition being "REALIST SCHIZOPHRENIA".

When two men are accused of murder, one does not seem to have known right from wrong, the other claims he knew just what he was doing. The one who does not know what he was doing is declared insane, while the other is sentenced to life imprisonment yet both are suffering from emotional illness. The only deference between the man declared insane and the man declared sane is the pretense roles in which they are trapped. The man declared insane is subject to erratic behavior and he regresses totally from reality, unconsciously he is trying to hive himself immunity to life by making himself unresponsible for his actions. The man declared sane is also playing a false role but he remains rational and his imaginary character, instead of denying his actions, condones them.

The person suffering from personality conflict can be just as smart and rational as any healthy person. The only way to tell them from the more healthy is by their behavior, by what they claim to believe, and lie detection methodology.

I am placing people with emotional illness into three main categories. DEPRESSIVES, REALISTS, AND ILLUSIONISTS. Realists are more rational than illusionists. Realists have created a false role for themselves In order to escape emotional suffering. Illusionists hide from conflicts by losing touch with reality, or control over their behavior. (Psychologically induced brain dysfunction accompanies illusionism).

For some one to have a Personality Conflict, that person would only have to disregard the fact that people he may persecute are unhappy, or that the people he associates with are also emotionally disturbed. This manipulation of communication in the brain is how a criminal can act one way when his emotions (ROM Language) would normally tell him not to. There is no doubt emotional illness is accomplished physically in the brain. This blocking out of information can create a variety of effects, in the criminally-ill it changes concepts of right and

p. 27

wrong to conform to the false character, this individual knows other people's definition for right and wrong, he will even claim to know the correct difference, but he truly does not consciously know the difference.

Some scientists believe that emotional illness will some day be cured with different drugs. Mental patients are being treated with drugs which calm the patient and stop him from having fits and since the original publication of this book drugs called neuroleptics have been used to decrease dopamine in patients witch has shown to decrees the hearing of voices and illusionism in patients.

Drugs are not going to ever solve the problem that caused a personality conflict. We have permanent true cures for emotional illness by placing the patient in touch with his true feelings with memory therapy and Psychoanalyses and improving his environment.

DEPROGRAMING UGLY HABITS
&
HAPPY BRAIN COORDINATION EXERCIZES

To exercise the Pineal Gland alone: hang a card on a wall with both sides distinguishably marked, turn the card over every half hour, only looking at a clock to check that you are doing it right.

To untangle your thoughts, make out a list of thoughts you had during the day to have the same thoughts the next day at the same times, try and figure out the origin of these thoughts and related thoughts you have had in the past memory images as well as goals. Consign a happy memory with each unhappy memory; don't avoid the unhappy memories or fears, not to suppress them. Remember your memories become your thoughts. Due to poor topical coordination we will mistake memories of other people's behavior as goal concepts and emulate that behavior even though that behavior would normally be disdainfully repulsive to us.

CHAPTER XVIII Emotional Illnesses and Symptoms

FEAR- is unhappiness combined with physical stress. Wheat affects the mind affects the body. Our bodies immediately after any sign of danger become electrically stimulated. The heartbeats faster, you would breathe faster and messages to the voluntary muscles speed up, this is to give us better reflexes and strength to avoid the trouble. When there is something we do not wish to happen:

p. 28

by frantically trying to think of a way to stop that event from occurring Fear is created.

PHOBIAS- are paranoid fears, which stem from past unpleasant events. When someone's lower consciousness is reminded of that event, the obsessive thought of that event forces the reoccurrence of fear that it will happen again.

The cure is in facing up to the symbol of the phobia by the patient's own volition; so that the person's subconscious will stop associating the symbol with the past event.

FEAR OF DEATH- The basic premise behind all phobias directly or indirectly is the fear of death: from fear of heights to fear of being laid off from your job, it is the fear of not continuing (of not being able to exist), the fear that as life changes death will come closer, and it will mean nonexistence. If we did not exist we could not regret not existing fear specifically fear of death is the confusion (depression) in the brain due to the conflict in terms (equations) based on conflicting observations with our ROM Language which is the wish to exist (to love everything existing) How can you love what would make it impossible to exist and love everything in existence. It is a paradox unless you assume that all living things are meant to eventually have eternal life, and what we actually love is all that will be in life in the future.

JEALOUSY- 1. Possessiveness caused by the fear of change, future, death, in other words (Fear of nonexistence, Yours or other individuals) 2. Later it comes out of the experience with exclusionism. 3. The RAM Program: To exist to be made happy by others; causes the depressed individual to feel abandoned by any loved one who can be happy or have friends while the jealous individual feels unhappy or alone do to Reoccurring Depression.

PARANOIA- is when the imagination is allowed to create answers to real questions, because of a communication problem between levels of consciousness. Illusions are mistaken for real life by the body, which reacts with fear, evoking an emotional response. Phobias are selective paranoia.

PREJUDICE- see chapter XVI Drugs, Gift to your teacher".

VANITY- is when someone considers himself better than other people, due to the false RAM Programming: The purpose in life is to be made happy by others. Or a more serious criminal schizophrenic role.

p. 29

SELF CONSIOUSNESS- paranoia from the RAM Language I must be made happy by others.

HATE- is not the opposite of love (which is the importance someone or thing has in your life) Hate is he mimicry of bullies believing being a member of a click will protect you from abuse. Or the belief that the removal of some one will protect your life.

OVERSENSITIVITY TO PAIN- Pain being the emotional response (confusion) to the neurological message that something is wrong and needs to be repaired. It is possible to learn to control pain and in some cases eliminate it without the use of drugs by feeling pain and through self hypnosis.

If you have broken a bone more than once in your life, then you have noticed how much less pain you had the second time around. I recommend a pain reliever to get to sleep. Sleep is important to healing.

This is a good place to remind people not to use pain relievers and sleeping pills at the same time and not to go to a second doctor without informing the first.

DEPRESSION- A slowing down of the brain, also confusion like pain only at a different place in the brain. A dwelling on an unsolvable paradox -- flooding neurons. A slowing down means more signals not less.

FUTURE SHOCK -- HOME SICKNESS- Are two names for depression. Caused by a feeling of LACK OF PURPOSE. We control our physiology, so in order to live we must wish to live, or life stops. In order to live and compute thoughts we must make sense of life. Just as each ant in a colony knows his purpose in life is to work in the colony, and his job depends on what he is physically designed for. We too feel a purpose in life. When your life style is changed suddenly by events which you cannot control, it is likely that you may become confused about your role in life, creating depression until you can re-evaluate your situation and regain a sense of purpose. Hostages acquire this type of depression, which can cause them to become brainwashed.

The depression of Homesickness is the fear of death of loved ones, and the fear that different parts of life will never be experienced again. The fear comes out of the biological clocks preprogrammed topical reminders, which act as thought inducers -- and the random element which thought is built upon. These thought reminders remind the homesick person of what he or she is missing rather than inducing awareness of present surroundings especially if the separation was unplanned and the individual has no immediate plans to stimulate his interest in his surroundings.   p. 30

To avoid depression a person may take on schizophrenic RAM Language (false explanation) for his depression such as believing it is a lack of personal control over his environment due to lack of wealth, and there is a conspiracy by people around him to keep him from his goals. People who have a similar Realist Schizophrenic role would become role modals. Since the role is false like a drug it never become fulfilling. Goal Seeking Realist Schizophrenia can cause chronic Manic Depression.

INSOMNIA- is the incorrect software programming of the biological clock such as Jet lag. We use more than one way to tell time habit stemming from the dopamine trigger determining memory and thought development and the Pineal Gland measurement of light. Sleeplessness can be caused by lack of serotonin to put the brain to sleep. Suppressed memory and anxiety of an impending event can cause sleeplessness. If the question is solely how to get to sleep then the therapy is to program the Hypothalamus through self hypnoses and an imaginary clock also by meditating at the time you should be sleeping for three nights in a row will usually cause you to fall asleep during that space of time the fourth night. Everyone should have a minimum of 8 hours of sleep.

PSYCHOSOMATIC ILLNESS- Due to a fixation caused by fear the subjects imaginings are so intense on the subject of an illness or pain, these imaginings are mistaken by the brain stem to be neuron sensory messages, therefore giving the individual the symptoms or potentially harmful allergic response of said disease. Rashes or premature hair loss due to stress.

HYPOCONDRIAC- some one who feels sympathetic (psychosomatic) pains due to the Phobic Fear of illness. Hypochondria are also a symptom of Manic Depression.

SUICIDES- People do not commit suicide because they wish to die; they commit suicide because they wish to live. Suicide is caused by severe depression; at the peaks of this depression the individual becomes fatigued or panicky which leads to irrational thought. Suicide is truly an effective way of gaining an affectionate, and supportive emotional response from people, the wish to obtain this affection causes the irrational act of suicide.

Suicide is also the result of false personalities (schizophrenia) where individuals have made suicide into a goal.

HALLUCINATIONS- are not psychological illness but mental illness psychological illness being programming, mental illness being damage to hardware of the brain. A good example of a psychological hallucination is when you look up at someone and for the first moment you see someone ells you thought it was going to be. Hearing voices and seeing things is do to the brain awakening chemical Norepenepherin not getting to all the brain as a result part of the brain is still asleep and dreaming the voices or sights.

BRAINWASHING- is the process of pressing someone into a false role by driving him to regress into his inner thoughts and in his outer consciousness he or she adopts an imaginary role to make life bearable.

The subconscious which controls the health of the body remains healthy while the conscious mind forms a defensive pretence role.

MANIC DEPRESSION- BEING THE IMOTIONAL ILLNESS AS APOSED TO THE MENTAL ILLNESS BIPOLAR DISEASE. The psychological illness shares the chemical imbalance of bipolar disease only is less intense this may be one emotional illness which causes a mental dysfunction; being, the chemical imbalance Bipolar Disease. Manic Depression is when an individual sensitive to depression becomes irrational in his haste not to feel the pain. A refusal to acknowledge the subject causing the depression is partially achieved by pretending there are other reasons or simply by concentrating on other thoughts. In Manic Depression the RAM Language: THE WISH TO BE LOVED BY OTHERS, degenerates into RAM Language: THE WISH TO BE MADE HAPPY BY OTHERS" The manic depressive can become addicted to the chemicals released by the brain when having a temper tantrum and the habit of the temper

p.32

tantrum or impulsive buying or impulsive cleaning is reinforced by repetition. A manic depressed person will blame the closest person for his depression and invent realist schizophrenic role playing reasons for his depression, which may be physical in origin or is do to a paradox in achieving ROM Language happiness.

BIPOLAR DISEASE- is the release of large quantities of neuro transmitters then the restriction of same alternately causing euphoria (manic nature), then a slowing down of the brain which can be perceived as depression. Psychiatrists often refer to bipolar disease as Manic Depression not acknowledging the software programming ailment I call Manic Depression these two diseases are similar but not the same.

SHYNESS, INSECURITY- The term "Anything that can go wrong will go wrong" expresses the RAM Language of insecurity. Shyness and insecurity work much like a phobia. It is the obsession with one's past mistakes in etiquette, combined with the phobic fear that they not only will not see their first friends again but that they are incapable of making or accepting new friends. Due to the wish to find new friends they start imagining they are at fault in not having more friends and as they obsessively recall past mistakes and unhappy occurrences regarding their past friendships, they are unintentionally programming their timework recall rhythms in the brain, (Review; Thoughts are patterns of recall. All associated with the pattern of signals in the brain at the time. After a certain length of time the messages would come full circle and reoccur. The pattern that reoccurs is held and compared with similar patterns, a compromise is accepted then released this new pattern will be compared with similar patterns and its existence changes the pattern, like coming to a repeat sign on music with alternate bars of music for the repeated music. Whenever the question or opportunity of making friends arises, so do the unpleasant memories and depression, to the exclusion of happy memories. These individuals may even begin to have delusions that they never had any friends, or would remember having a fight with a friend but not that they made up. As a result the insecurity of shyness would case the individual to fear or avoid (due to depression) social events, or friend making opportunities.

NYMPHOMANIA- is an addiction to the rush of neurotransmitters first encountered from the excitement of the first encounter. The choice comes from the false RAM Language to be made happy by others which degenerates to lack of sexual activity to be the cause of depression denying insecurity, overcoming shyness, and adopting reoccurring depression in place of constant depression.

CHAPTER IXX Cure must relate to cause

p. 33

Psychological analysis and Psychiatric care cannot take place without acknowledging that the following is inherent knowledge: The wish to love everything (the wish to be happy), The knowledge of immortality (after life).

The cure for emotional illness is related to the cause. By looking at the factors in the cause of emotional illness we can create a therapy to cure it.

(a) A "Realist Schizophrenic (Personality Conflict) is the creation of an imaginary role, therefore to give credibility to that role would only reinforce the patient's role playing. Placing criminals behind bars or telling them they are going to be punished reinforces their false role. Placing a patient in contact with other people suffering from Realist Schizophrenia would also reinforce his false role (Emotional Realist Schizophrenia is not to be confused with psychiatric Schizophrenia which is a chemical imbalance).

(b) Emotional suffering causes emotional illness, therefore an improved environment is needed. Conflicts between ROM L. And RAM L. in the patients would then work to cure them. Brainwashing is usually a part of emotional conflicts. Someone who is brainwashed is emotionally ill and unstable. Brain washing or torture would not work to cure the patient.

(c) The past experiences of the patients have a great deal to do with their present condition. And in their past lies their last truly healthy thoughts and emotions. By remembering their past they can get in touch with their true aspirations and realize that the roles they play are not really theirs. Righting a biography, talking to a therapist about the past (incorporating the memories of others to induce memory), in extreme circumstances memories can be induced by sodium pentothal (sodium-pentothal also causes memory loss when it wares off so the remembered events and thoughts must be repeated to the person over and over till those memories are recalled or an acceptance of them is achieved.

(d) Many times criminals received a lack of sensitivity, and physical abuse from others, which contributed to their emotional illness. So it is important that people show the subjects that they care about what happens to them.

(e) The committing of a crime to show solidarity and loyalty to a gang is to solicit affection (acceptance). A criminal often is doing the same thing, through a proxy gang or role model he has seen in the street, or famous criminals he tries to relate to; he creates make believe friends. This is why a majority of crimes are copycat crimes, yet another reason to keep the criminally ill separated within a rehabilitation institution.

p 34

(f) Our prisons must be turned into hospitals with daily psychoanalyses. There must be a theater in the prison where plays depicting pitfalls for the patients are shown, and religious guidance made available.

Dear sirs: Many people have died from lack of sleep. Remember God has a plan for us and others care for us even strangers! Do not take your life by accident or on porpoise by taking muscle relaxants and sleeping pills or other drugs. This is from "The Brain" to get over insomnia meditate three nights the fourth night you should fall asleep at the same time you were meditating, get some one to hold you down if you have to, to de sensitize your self to pain it is important to take few pain relievers but an aspirin, Tylenol, or moltram just before bed and only if your in pain may help you to get to sleep which is very important to the heeling process don't self medicate don't go to more than one doctor unless they are conferring with each other and as a scientist I can tell you not to trust a doctor who prescribes many types of medication, and at the moment Neuroliptics are being over prescribed when only a small dose is necessary in most cases if it does not work a larger does will not work ether. Question your pharmacist about all the medications you are taking at once often they are better trained than the Doctor. If sleepless-ness persists I strongly endorse Psychotherapy it works and it should be in the schools and our prisons. Apathy and denial have kept these true cures from being made use of, hens the original name of my book "Confusion? or Apathy!". Many of your favorite stars have died from sleeplessness Merlin Monrow, Elvis Prestly, Michael Jackson, The Joker from Bat Man and many more- most of these were accidental deaths. An acquaintance of mine only 21 was over prescribed Respiridal which killed that individual yet I still hear doctors claim it is safe in large doses even though it is a powerful chemical and only a little is necessary. So Please be aware and Proactive in your own treatment.

MECHANISM OF U.S. INFLATION

This article is to dispel some wide spread myths about the economy, such as the myth that increased supply of money creates inflation, and decreased supply creates deflation. With decreased supply of money, prices are raised to make up for the loss in sales; less goods are sold for the same revenue, and any natural boycott as a result of higher prices, fails. Deflation can only occur during a severe depression. Increased supply of money does not cause any inflation; since greed is countered by competition.

The name economist is misleading, economists do not study our economy they study the monetary system and other related systems, as designed by their authors. These rightfully called themselves economists. Most things on earth are perfection, but many things we do as homosapiens are not perfection. The fear that perfection does not exist has caused some people to deny the existence of perfection; in order to escape the fear. This is one reason economists refuse to study the economy as it exists. The reason economists came to the conclusion, increased supply of money causes inflation, was because it gave a simplified argument in be half of small government, and a perfect monetary system. Deflation occurred during a time of small government, inflation is occurring now and the government is large; this is where study on the part of economists came to a stop. The government grew in order to better fulfill its purpose, (which is to keep the greatly and partially emotionally disturbed from harming themselves or other people) bureaus were

p 38

created such as the F.B.I., Department of the Interior, Environmental Protection Agency, and the Food and Drug Administration...,. There has been a growing number of people who resent: environmental, consumer, and safety regulations, these people where told that these regulations cause inflation.

Regulations do not affect competition there for can not cause recession. Recession-- is when a significant number of people have the price of their bills rising faster than their salary, or when a significant number of people are unemployed. The threat of price controls has also invoked a radical conservative view. Price controls are the removal of decision making from millions of people (each of whom places a great deal of effort and expertise into there decisions) and places these decisions into the hands of a few. The economy is simple to understand, but it is an understatement to say our economy is very complex in detail.

There is no such thing as production falling behind demand with out the aid of war, or population shift. Population shift is the greatest cause of inflation, it is caused by poverty when combined with the construction of highways for growth, or recreation., Poor aesthetic planning, and unfriendly rivalry between states, and between cities. During the sixties, recession from population shift was held back by huge expenditures by the government, which boosted sales. When government expenditures dropped in the 70s relative to the number of services being received and the number of jobs provided; it had a hard hitting impact on the strained economy. Inflation is also caused by: Discriminatory grants to private businesses; Attempts by the U.S. Treasury Dept. to lower inflation by decreasing the availability of money; Inflationary expenditures by the government; The use of gold and silver mine industries to distribute new money; and by giving discriminatory grants, and loans for market related technology and growth, the government creates a higher income bracket where there is no market for it. Government grants for Technological research is unconstitutional since it is discriminatory against individuals, and against other companies; which would benefit from developing and gaining patent to said Technology. Most companies evolve out of one patent. Two companies producing the same amount as one company employs almost twice as many people. The less companies there are, the fewer jobs there are. Government grants to private industry is a monopolizing strategy.

The department of the U.S. Treasury has caused a great deal of inflation by suppressing the supply of money to control inflation. Borrowing is almost the same as saving, instead of saving a little at a time, you spend a little at a time, the interest can be inflationary. Because of the belief by economists that increased supply of money causes inflation, the government may cause interest rates to be above what the banks need to sustain themselves (creating inflation). When bank reserves became low it indicates that the government did not create enough money; since the overwhelming majority do not take loans they cannot pay back. By using only one industry (precious metal mining) to distribute money, the money is more slowly and unevenly distributed. p 40

Before and during World War One, the U.S. was the leading exporter. After World War One, countries started making their own products which were supplied manly by the United States in the past, and they started consuming less. This combined with North Americas worst drought and poor conservation, devastated the economy. The monetarists saw the declining productivity, and stopped printing money, but failed to stop the population from growing. Prices lowered during the depression because there was little diversity in income brackets, and percentage wise unemployment was many times what it is today (before the crash of 1929 took place).

When the government takes over an industry which is or may come to be commercial; the government crates inflation, by lowering employment and eliminating competition. This inflation makes it very difficult for that industry to again become self sufficient. In the case of education, retirement funds, and employment of he poor...; the government needs to step in, to fulfill the purpose of having a government (as stated earlier). The post office roads and telephone poles maybe even airports are necessary infrastructure to allow free enterprise to exist.

Our government is a non profit association with which we are members. With In this organization the law of supply and demand is replaced by the democratic process. In the United States productivity is potentially limitless there fore if something is desperately needed, politicians will not be put off by insufficient revenue. The expenditure of deficit money does not in itself create inflation, the expenditure of inflationary payments creates inflation. If the government would compare their contracts with private contracts in a different field but with a similar work force, work hours, and with similar materials; to obtain a price estimate, and be legally bound to boycott any price which exceeds that estimate; the government would be mimicking the commercial market place. Its deficit then could have no adverse impact on the economy. If every one were allowed to make their own money, it would eliminate the purpose of having an economic system (which is to compel the partially emotionally ill to do their share of work). In our system the emotional illness, greed is controlled by competition. The democratic system keeps the government running as efficiently as possible. If the government can mimic the commercial sector in it's expenditures, and refrain from competing with potential commercial enterprises, the government can be allowed to print it's own money. This would also connect the printing of money with actual economic growth, and would allow its prompt and even distribution.

Arhur P. Vavoudis

Independent Psychological Researcher

SOLAR INDUSTRIES CO. JOURNAL NO.1

Written by

Arthur P. Vavoudis

p. 44 THE FIRST AFFORDABLE SOLAR PANEL FOR NEW ENGLAND WINTER USE! Pays for itself in two years.

Copyright 1982 by Arthur P. Vavoudis

THE FIRST AFFORDABLE SOLAR PANEL FOR NEW ENGLAND WINTER USE!

$5.35 a sq. ft. including installation. Pays for itself in two years. 100% systems only (from 1982 best seller reprinted as solution journal 1987 Solar Industries never got off the ground.)

It is efficient enough for winter use since it has strong vacuum insulation. The unique and exclusive features which make this panel affordable are: that the exterior body of the panel is made out of Acrylic Thermoplastic. Acrylic thermoplastic is stronger than glass; meaning less material is needed for the desired strength, than would be needed if glass were used; making thermoplastic cheaper than both glass and aluminum. The use of thermoplastic was made possible by separating the collector plate from the exterior of the panel with a strong vacuum; and by separating the pipe from the exterior of the panel with insulated washers. To cut the weight and material costs of the panel even further, painted aluminum foil is used as the collector surface. The foil is stretched between two pipes; rubber construction putty separates the foil and pipe, and conducts heat between the two, this is to prevent corrosion due to contact between the two different metals; it also aids in quick assembly. The Aluminum Foil glued so that it holds the construction putty in place. Because of the panel's light weight,, and the safety in handling the making and installation of the panel is much cheaper, (27 ounces a sq. ft.). The Acrylic Thermoplastic used is the same used in eyeglasses. The inner faces of the acrylic windows have ridges across the length of the inner faces of the panel which protrude in arcs. This is to increase surface area therefore increasing the amount of reflection on the inside of the panel. The exterior faces of the panel remain flat in order to allow as little reflection as possible. The inner surfaces of acrylic are coated with an infrared reflectance to keep heat from irradiating out of the panel.

Solar Industries is not ready for production yet, but if you wish to be at the head of the line in obtaining our panels send your name and address to:xxxxxxxxxxxxxxxxxxxxx When we are prepared to take orders we will get in touch with you on a first come first serve basis. Our goal is to retrofit 90% of all buildings in the United States with our panels by 1985.

MECHANISM OF INFLATION

p 45

The Federal Reserve Board is increasing our interest rates because they claim that increased availability of money causes inflation and decreased availability of money creates deflation. Greater demand than supply which does cause inflation comes from times of war and Population Shift; when the growth or population of one community starts moving to another area this causes disorganization allowing many markets to be temporarily untapped and wide open. This prolonged condition allows inflation to go rampant. A sudden increase In the availability of money can create greater demand than supply in some luxury products but most always shortages will not occur long enough to cause [price increases. The Federal Reserve Board increases interest rates because they claim increased availability of money is the same as greater demand than supply; since the deficit creates a greater supply of money than the Federal Reserve has decided is needed, they increase interest rates (this is supposed to lower inflation by decreasing the availability of money). Lowered availability of money causes inflation not deflation if a business man or woman loses his customers with a certain income, an individual is not going to lower his prices to regain those customers; he has no control of the expenses he must pay or the investment he may already have spent. A recession is a scramble to stabilize wages and prices. In a recession where wages and prices are falling the added disorganization can be well compared to running backwards and we would quickly spiral into a depression. Half of the population makes several thousand dollars a year more than the other half, this slows down the recessional affect of inflation, allowing more time for recovery of wage and price balance. Stores can not attract customers which do not exist

p. 46

by lowering prices; this is the case with lowered availability of money (lowered sales) population, businesses, or employment.

Population Shift is caused by: The construction of highways for growth and recreation, Poor aesthetic planning, enlarged sewer systems, tax incentives specifically designed to promote population shift, and land speculators (investors). The objective of land speculation is to make a profit from inflation, land is purchased in an area which is growing in population, then the land is held undeveloped and with the aid of other land investors a shortage of developed land is created making property much more valuable; meaning the price is jacked up. Land speculation also involves getting involved in politics to: Get highways built near or along your property., Getting your property zoned so that it will bring the highest price possible., To increase the sewer capacity of the city., And create tax incentives and subsidies, to get businesses to move to the city in which your property is located. Our Government is so pro land speculation and uncontrolled growth that most speculators believe they are improving the economy when in reality they have been destroying it.

The government has created a great deal of inflation by suppressing the availability of money to control inflation. Borrowing is almost the same as saving; instead of saving a little at a time, You spend a little at a time the amount of money changing hands does not change, and money is only removed from banks for short periods of time. When bank reserves become low it indicates that the government did not create enough money, because the overwhelming majority do not take loans they cannot pay back.

By using only one industry (precious metal mining) to distribute new money, the money is at first unevenly distributed therefore it's effect on he economy is too slow and inflationary.

Inflation is also caused by: Discriminatory grants to private businesses, and Inflationary expenditures by the government.

By giving discriminatory grants and loans for market related technology and growth, the government creates a higher income bracket where there is no market for it. Government grants for Technological Research are unconstitutional since it is discriminatory against individuals, and other companies which would benefit from developing and gaining patent to said Technology. Most companies evolve out of one patent, Two companies producing the same amount as one company employs almost twice as many people. Government grants to private industry is a monopolizing strategy. Unemployment causes inflation through lowered availability of money.

When the government takes over an industry which is or may come to be commercial, the government is creating inflation, by lowering employment and eliminating competition. This inflation makes it very difficult for that industry to again become self sufficient. In the case of education retirement funds, and employment of the poor,...; the government needs to step in, to fulfill the purpose of having a government.

p. 48

Taken from the Federal Reserve Bank of Atlanta
Economic Review July/August 1980

Monetary Policy and Interest Rates by Robert

Chart 2

**1975-78 period showed that falling interest rates
do not always accompany a depreciating dollar**

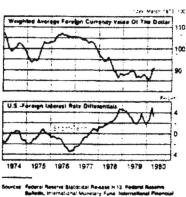

Sources: Federal Reserve Statistical Release H.13 Federal Reserve
Bulletin, International Monetary Fund International Financial
Statistics
*Secondary market rates for 90-day large certificates of deposit in the
United States less the weighted average of foreign three-month money
market rates

The fact that higher inflation rates coincided with
rates, and that those higher interest did not resul
slowing down of inflation; is confirmed by the char
which show food prices rising with interest rates.
Taken from the Federal Reserve Bulletin No.1, Vol.5

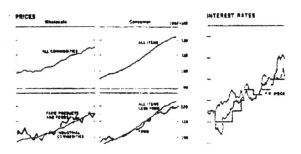

Figure 1. Growth of Money and Federal Debt*
1960-1978

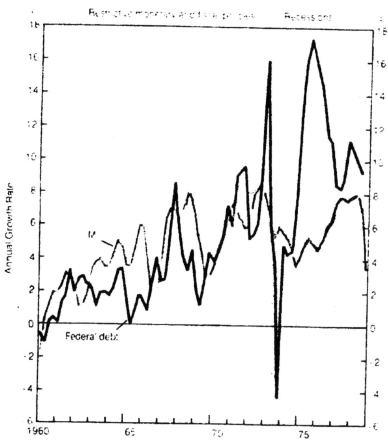

*Money is a 3 quarter moving average of M. Federal debt is a 3 quarter moving average of the total interest bearing federal public debt.

p. 50

Figure 2. Rate of Inflation
(GNP Deflator 1960-1978)

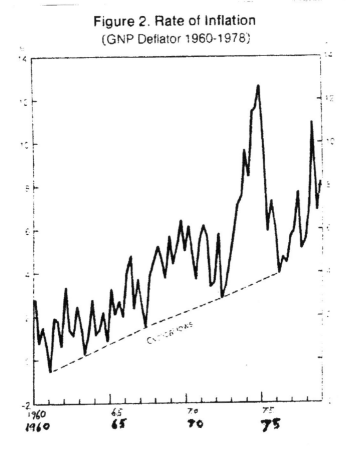

p. 51

Taken from the Federal Reserve Bank of Atlanta
Economic Review July/August 1980
Monetary Policy and Interest Rates by Robert E. Keleher

Chart 2

1976-78 period showed that falling interest rates
do not always accompany a depreciating dollar.

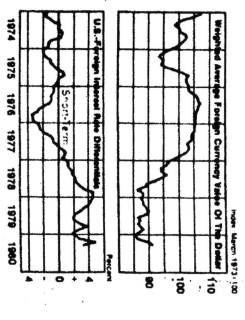

Weighted Average Foreign Currency Value Of The Dollar

Index March 1973=100

110

100

90

U.S.-Foreign Interest Rate Differentials

Short-term

Percent

+4

+2

0

-2

-4

1974 1975 1976 1977 1978 1979 1980

Sources: Federal Reserve Statistical Release H.13; Federal Reserve
Bulletin; International Monetary Fund, International Financial
Statistics
'Secondary market rates for 90-day, large certificates of deposit in the
United States less the weighted average of foreign three-month money
market rates.

p. 52

Before and during World War 1, the U.S. was the leading exporter. After WW1, countries started importing less, this combined with North America's worst drought to create high unemployment, and lower productivity. Monetarists thought the printing of money represented growth in demand when in reality it represented growth in productivity and population. Monetarists assumed lower production meant there would be a shortage of goods. If it had created a shortage of goods the law of supply and demand would have raised prices rationing goods without the aid of lower money production.

Prices lowered during the depression because the shortage of money was excessive. A constitutional amendment to balance the federal budget would result in another grate depression.

The government grew in size in order to better fulfill it's purpose, (which is to keep the greatly and partially emotionally disturbed from harming themselves or other people) bureaus were created such as the F.B.I., Department of the Interior, Environmental Protection Agency, and the food and Drug Administration,... There has been a growing number of people who resent: Environmental, Consumer, and Safety regulations; These people were told that these regulations cause inflation Regulations which keep the partially emotionally ill from harming themselves or other people, cannot cause recession since they do not interfere with competition, and any increase in expense is balanced by an increase in employment.

p. 53

Our government is a non profit association with which we are members. With in this organization the law of supply and demand is replaced by the democratic process. In the United States productivity is potentially limitless therefore if something is desperately needed, politicians will not be dissuaded by insufficient revenue. The expenditure of deficit money does not in itself create inflation, the expenditure of inflationary payments creates inflation. If the government would compare their contracts with private contracts in a different field but with a similar work force, work hours, and with similar materials, to obtain a price estimate; and be legally bound to boycott any price which exceeds that estimate; the government would then be mimicking the commercial market place therefore its deficit would not have any adverse impact on the economy. If everyone were allowed to make their own money it would eliminate the purpose of having an economic system (which is to compel the partially emotionally ill to do their share of work). In our system the emotional illness greed is controlled by competition. The Democratic System keeps the government running as efficiently as possible. If the government can mimic the commercial sector in its expenditures, and refrain from competing with potential commercial enterprises; the government can be allowed to print its own revenue. This would also connect the printing of money with Technological and Populace growth, and would allow [prompt and even distribution of new money.

Emotional illness is caused by emotional stress which would otherwise cause physical illness, if it were not for the minds ability to play tricks on it's

The fact that higher inflation rates coincided with higher interest rates, and that those higher interest did not result in a significant slowing down of inflation; is confirmed by the charts below; which show food prices rising with interest rates.

Taken from the Federal Reserve Bulletin No.1, Vol.58, January 1972

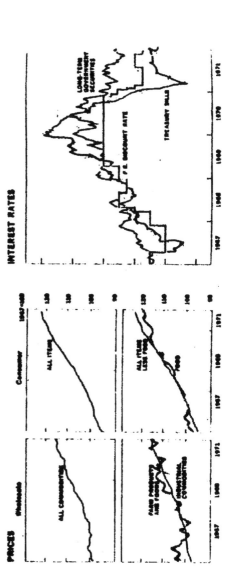

self by creating false personalities, delusions, loss of memory, and by manipulating the attention span. Any amount of stress no matter how small causes an equal intensity of emotional illness. The fact that no other economist has arrived at the conclusion in this article is partly do to there reluctance to acknowledge that we have an economic system solely because of the need to control mental illness; they like to think of the trade system as being necessary to organize adequate production to meat demand, because of the complexity of this task; in reality if it were not for emotional illness we would determine what is needed and would produce it for each other no strings attached. But presently this is not possible because of the extent of emotional illness.

Over simplified pessimistic theories which dominate economics today, were also promoted by the threat of price controls. People did not know how to respond to this threat so as a defense they adopted the false principles of Libertarianism, which is that the government should be restricted to regulating violent and theft crimes only.

Price controls would create a depression; goods, services, and resources must be rationed according to need; the law of supply and demand does this by price, the scarcer a material is the more it must cost. A material with more than one use must have a greater price than its more common or less used substitute, in order to keep that substance available to the uses in which there is no substitute. Prices must change as technology and chance cause availability of goods and services to change. Even the uses of materials can

p. 56

change rapidly. If spinach growers have a bad season and the price does not rise, only people close to the source could obtain spinach and the farmers may go bankrupt; but if the price rises any one who has not had spinach for a while and wishes to supplement his meal with spinach, it would be available to him at the higher price which that individual under normal circumstances can afford. This does not apply to the poor, but with the aid of this article poverty can be eliminated. The government can not regulate prices; it is easy to understand how the economy works but it is an understatement to say the economy is very complex in detail.

2009 insert When I heard people advocating the flat tax I new our economy would be destroyed. And greed is even more pronounced than I thought. Income tax on the wealthy has always been high but they were not paying that much because there were deductions for Building, Manufacturing, and hiring within the United States of America. With out these incentives I predicted all our jobs would go over seas and to Canada and Mexico and this is exactly what has happened and we are now currently in a Depression not recession but a Depression.

p 57

The Federal Reserve Bank of Cleveland's 1981 Annual Report, p.8-9 Charts 6-5 confirmed Chart 2 and Figures 1 and 2.

A chart in the Federal Reserve Bank of New York Monthly Review 1964 Vol.46 No.9 p. 178 Chart 1, when compared to a Chart in the Federal Reserve Bank of New York Monthly Review 1964 Vol.46 No11 Chart 3 p.216 it is shown that a sharp increase in money production with steady interest rates, do not impede strong growth in production.

During 1949-50 a sharp decrease in bank credit was not countered by higher interest rates as a result sales and production increased unimpeded. Ref. Federal Reserve Bulletin Feb. 1954 Vol.40 No.2 p.145 Industrial production Chart, p.150 Bank Credits Chart. Federal Reserve Bulletin Dec. 1954 Vol. 40 No. 12 p.1249 Selected Short Term Mortgage Rates.

Between 1951-53 interest rates were sharply increased causing a drop in production, increased government employment' offset an extreme inflationary reaction. Ref. Federal Reserve Bulletin May 1954 Vol.40 No.5 p. 462 Price and trade Charts; Federal Reserve Bulletin Aug. 1954 Vol.40 No.8 p.805 p.810 Employment Charts, p.811 Unemployment Chart.

Increased interest rates are followed by an increase in the number of bankruptcies filed. Ref. Federal Reserve Bank of Cleveland Economic Review Spring/1982 p.11 fig.6 Chart on bankruptcies between 1970 and 1975.

Federal Reserve Bank of New York, Monthly Review Nov. 1964 vol.46 No.11 Reflections on the Early Development of Open Market Policy by W. Randolph Burgess p. 219-226 explains the events which led up to the Depression of 1929; but mistakenly blames interest rates being too low to suppress growth in which there was not enough money to support. Rather than blaming the lack of money to support growth which had enough manpower and production to be maintained.

Federal Reserve Bank of New York Monthly Review 1964 Vol. 46 No.9 Chapter 1. p.178 when compared to Federal Reserve Bank of New York Jan. 1964 vol.46 No.1 Chart 1, p.15 it shows lower interest rates increase production.

Federal Reserve Bulletin Apr.1954 vol.40 No.4 Charts on Construction Contracts p. 347' when compared with Charts on Industrial Production same page, peak construction periods (which would denote population shift) coincide with a drop in production.

NON PROFIT SMALL BUSINESS LOAN BANK

Solar Industries will in the future be funding a non profit bank which will eliminate poverty in third world nations The bank will give no collateral loans to the chronically unemployed for starting a small business. The bank will keep the size of the loans low by hiring and training people to produce the materials needed by he companies in question. Using outdated patents, and social workers the bank will seek out and enlist people into acquiring loans to create products and services which are not being provided, or are not being provided at a price which is affordable to peop;le with a low income. The price of goods sold by the loan recipient will be determined by the bank; export and import will be prohibited. The purpose of this is to create a healthy trade system between the lower income population, raising their standard of living. The standard of living will rise as unemployment declines, then restrictions on trade can be lifted causing the foreign value of their dollars to increase; but more important there will be a large native market and the difference between income levels would be greatly diminished. The most common wage in a country will be considered the minimumwage, the interest payment will only be required on months in which the loan recipient earns more than the minimum wage and the interest will be 20% of the money in exess to the minimum wage until the loan plus 10% is payed back; if the recipeint never earns more than the minimum he will never owe anything to the bank. All requests for educational loans will be granted; an education is always a good investment. (update: This is wishfull thinking maybe a guide).

p.60

ENERGY OPTIONS AND THEIR EFFECT ON THE ENVIRONMENT

The first fact in the energy issue is that we have enough options so that we do not need to: pollute the air, Couse adverse climatic changes be increasing the percentage of corbondioxide in the air., De-stroy our fresh water aquatic life with acid rain due to sulfur in the air., Destroy vast amounts of land and ground water systems in mining coal and oil shale., Increase disease in aquatic life by increasing radiation in Aquatic Habitats., Destroy large habitats by obstructing the water flow in a way which floods wild life habitat or stops migration of aquatic life.l, It is not necessary to eliminate habitat for many birds, small mammals, specialized plants, and insects, by cutting dead or aging trees for fire wood. The second fact is that we are doing all of he above and that this destruction must be stopped not accelerated.

Wood is not a suitable energy source; our present and past oil supplies where created from several hundred million generations of aquatic life, one generation of life on land does not come near the size of one generation of life on land does not come near the size of one generation of aquatic life. Oil burns many times more efficiently than wood therefore when used properly oil creates less air pollution; with the exception of sulfur which can be remove from oil. In the past there was also a trend to add pollution causing agents to the oil so that its burning qualities would cater to the engines performance, fortunately this trend has been reversed, now engines are being designed to cater to the performance of the oil; with cleaner air and better mileage as a result. There is still room for a great deal more improvment in fuel burning technology for more efficient use of fuel; partially burned oil is a dangerous poison and a waste of fuel.

Tree farm waste is not an aceptable substitute fuel; when this so-called waste is great enough not to be needed as mulch for the next crop, it is used for: Portical Board, Paper, Plastics, and Chemicals.

Garbage is a legitimate source of energy which should be made use of. Garbage on the bottom of the Atlantic off New Jerseys coast produced so much methane gas that when unstable chemicals or chemical set it off it blew up with the force of an Atomic Bomb; this is only one example of destrutive waste.

The failure to recycle glass, metals, and plastics, is another great waste of fuel. The fusion of ingredients of glass, the refining of metl oars, and the making of plastics, all take more energy than remelting and molding of he finished product. Stripmineing of metal oar and silica is costly to our energy supply of oil and it is costly to or environment.

Coal creates more corbondioxide than oil; in order to convert coal to Cynfuels, and to remove sulfur from coal; a great deal of energy needs to be exhausted making Cynfuels expensive. Coal burns less efficiently than oil causing more air pollution. A large amount of land is being destroyed by stripmineing. The surface of the earth is made up of five main layers; soil is only a thin shell on the surface of the Earth (the thickness and types of the different soils varies greatly). Strip Mines are dug from 90 to 300 feet deep, once this mass of rock is turned over the sediment and organic soil only peper the rubble. The breaking up of the mantle turns the ground into a sponge which soaks up rain and causes the water tables to drop out of the reach of the roots of plants, dereases the size of above ground water channels, and causes the leaching of sulfur into the water table. In order to truly reclaim land, an asphalt blanket needs to be laid below the sediment to keep the water table from sinking too quickly. Each of the first three layers should have been saved and kept separate in a way which would keep them from eroding away. Each layer needs to be placed back where it was, and native vegetation planted and watered if necessary in order to avoid erosion. This will not stop our energy bills from rising. In places where the layers of stone are over 100 feet thick strip mining becomes impractical economically; this is one of the reasons underground mining is still the dominant source of coal. Underground mining still pollutes ground water and the coal mine contains sulfur and phosphorus which will end up in our air unless the coal is converted into synthetic fuels and these chemicals removed. This would guarantee to raise our fuel prices. Obviously greater use of coal should be only a last resort, yet it's use is being promoted now.

The oil embargo caused gas lines not because there was a shortage of American oil reserves but because there was a shortage of production which would have been felt toward the end of that winter, if the embargo had lasted that long. The lines could have been avoided if the oil companies had tried a little harder but then they would have been passing up the chance to convince the public of the importance of: oil price decontrol, (which I agree with) energy conservation to a small degree, and the need for the government to throw money their way. Any business is a profitable business when you're awarded large or almost limitless capital by the govenment, this is why unpopular (destructive) energy sources have become so popular with corporations. Oil corporations have also been calling for greater use of our domestic oil supplies now, in case we are cut off by the Arab Nations in the future; it is a lot less profitable to say we need increased oil production potential.

Geothermal energy is estimated to be more abundent than coal and the cleanest energy source along with solar.

The United States has enough oil reserves to last one hundred years at todays rate of consumption and I predict that twenty times that amount will be found at greater depths when technology makes it possible and environmentally safe. For drilling in shallower water, safe oil rigs have been designed but the oil companies fight against their use. Oil tankers are not safe, they do not have enough maneuverability and their structure is not strong enough in proportion to their weight A tanker will sink itself if it strikes a solid obstacle when moving 10 miles an hour. There are no oil tankers with adaquate collision warning systems. If you wish to know how 38% of our oil reserves are being made inaccessible by negligent oil recovery methods read the article on Geopressure Wells. p. 64

Wind Power: Many huge wind mills could cause climatic changes, but smaller wind mills will contribute a great deal in saving energy.

Wave Power: The obstruction of waves close to shore is very damaging to costle ecology and aquatic life, but a few far off shore power plants can contribute before becoming obsolete.

Atomic: Our atomic technology is primitive and design deficient. In the future new materials and techniques will make control of radiation and the recycling of waste 100% efficient. For now the construction of new atomic Plants should be banned, and methods of collecting leaks rather than allowing them to escape, must be built into existing reactors.

Hydroelectric Power: dams destroy entire ecosysems and flood large amounts of valuable land. In Egypgt over one hundred square miles has been floodedl. The use of non restrictive flow hydroelectric plants which will be more efficient than present dams; is not a new concept, just overdue.

Solar Power: The Silicon Photovaltaic Cell which changes light into electricity seems very desirable due to its expense, and the attention it receives from the press; actually its high price is due to missing technology in it's manufacture. The Silica Photovaltaic Solar Cell is actually very inefficient compared to heat collecting Solar Panels. The strongest photovaltaic cells have an efficiency of 18% while the weakest thermal solarpanels can get 30% efficiency. Solar Industries is about to bring the world into the age of solar power. I have designed the first affordable solar panel for New England Winter use. Our definition of affordable is that a 100% solar heating system would pay for itself in two to three years, while any other 100% system would pay for itself in no less than 15 years. Solar Industries goal is to retrofit 90% of all buildings in the United States with solarpanels by 1985. (update I placed my solar panel in public domain with this publication 1982).

UNDERGROUND GEOPRESSURED LAKES AN ENERGY SOURCE BEING WASTED!

Water trapped underground and under thousands of tons of [pressure is being proposed for use in slurry pipelines and more have been proposed. This is a tremendous waste incomparison to its other uses. Geoprissure could be used in Tertiary removal of oil fom wells, in order to recover a large part of the 68% of oil which can not be recovered using regular methods. Our oil wells can only remove oil toward the drill entrance; as the pressure decreases, surrounding earth collapses silt and ruble obstructs the flow of oil. Pumping the oil also takes a large amount of energy. By piping water under pressure into oil wells before and during pumping, more oil can be removed.

I strongly endorse the use of Geopressure Water in obtaining enegy from geothermal wells; in this way the largest electric power plants on earth could be built.

The water does contain poisonous compounds but they are biodegradable and the water is quicly and inesxpensively cleaned, with the chemicals taking a harmless form, making this water a legitimate source for irrigating crops.

With use of coal slurry pipelines most of this valuable energy will be wasted and the water polluted with sulfur and phosphorous which are not very biodegradable.

Book Preview

CONFUSION? OR APATHY!

A CLEAR DEFINITION OF PSYCHOLOGY

AND

THE FIRST REHABILITATION PROGRAM

FOR CONVICTED CRIMINALS

To this day no government hase recognised crime as a product of mental illness. There fore there has never been an attempt to rehabilitate criminals under sentence. Programs meant to educate, and encourage ex-criminals from returning to a life of crime are very rare and under funded, this includes programs for juvenile affenders. Due to the apathy toward depressing subjects. A large number of mental patients who can not afford an expensive Psychiatrist are being warehoused in mental hospitals. Everyone has experienced slight amounts of each existing type of emotional illness. Since I

P. 67

was three years old I wished to know why there is such a thing as suffering therefore I have been studying emotional illness in my self, and my father ever since. By comparing emotional illness in myself to more serious cases; I was able to explain in this book, how the mind works, and what criminal illness is; I have proposed the first Criminal Rehabilitation Program, and I have set necessary guidelines for the creation of such programs. (update I invented the turm Nuerophysicist I turned this book into a book of how the mind and brain work and most of the discoveries are my own the present name of the book is The Brain by Nuerophysicist Arthur P. Vavoudis what I was working for was to find a cure of role playing wich leeds to criminality, meaness, or violence and verbal abuse of families and I did discover the cure it was allready known it is Psychotherapy now lets put it to use in schools and prisons it would reduce crime in america and much sufering at leest 99%).

TO SAVE THE CALIFORNIA CONDOR AND OTHERS

The purpose of this article is to give an understanding of how to raise baby birds in captivity without causing emotional deprivation which leads to both physical and emotional illness. By having this knowledge birds endangered of extinction can be saved by collcting eggs in the wild. Female birds remain fertile for the entire breeding season in order to replace eggs which preditors have eaten; this is a natural fact of life in the life of a bird and it is not frustrating as long as the mother succeds in raising a brood that season During the ninteenth century egg collectors (egg colleting from nests is now illegal) reported collecting up to 136 eggs from single nests. There is one thorough report by an egg collector in the American Naturalist Magz. May 1, 1868, vol.2 p.382 no.7; where he collected 31 Goden Winged Woodpecker eggs from one nest, by weekly removing all but two eggs out of what was originally a clutch of six eggs. The bird continually laid more eggs to maintain the original number, and did not stop until the original two eggs left in the nest hatched. Leaving two eggs probably helped keep the bird from abandoning the nest and being in the wild made the idea of losing eggs more natural. If the bird was in aptivity and all of the eggs were removed, she would feel that she had less control over the situation, and may abandon her efforts.

The idea of using such a method to save endangered birds became controversial with the death of a number of birds being raised in captivity, two of which were California Condor chicks. These two chicks are a good example of how not to raise baby birds. They were fed by an automatic mechanism, were kept on screening instead of a nest; and in every way they were treated like objects instead of living things.

In order to raise wild birds in captivity first the chicks will need the security, love and sustenance from parents which are familier to them. In some cases a puppet parent is used to make the circumstances seem more natural, but just the same the chicks know that there is a human being who cares about them working the puppet. If the puppet is mechanical, and the birds are not fed by hand, it would cause emotional deprivation to occur. The puppet is a good idea but occasional sight contac of adults of their own species is adequate to keep the chicks from becoming overly weary of their own kind. Human Beings are adequate substitute parents, these parents must be familiar to the birds from the time they hatch. Twenty-four hours should not pass without the birds seeing all the parents once. The pertuxent condor research center has developed the idea of covering the birds at night so that they do not miss the presence of their parents at that time. A parent must always be present during the day in order to promote a sense of security and the use of their senses. It is absolutely necessary that the birds be hand fed so that they feel the hand directly or through an eyedropper or tongs; by this I mean the movement of the living hand is felt through the utensil being held, and the body heat of the parent would be felt. No automatic feeding devices are acceptable. The particular species of bird being raised may have a certain form of behavior to let the mother know it's hungry. This behavior must be promoted when raising birds in captivity. The chicks must be raised in a nest and if the species being raised are meant to be raised in the open the chicks must not be kept in a very confined space. Instinct is the combination of physical ability and inborn taste but for this to result in the correct behavior the chicks must be taught. If the chicks are raised on screening it would make nest building more difficult for them to learn; and if a species which is normally raised in the open is raised in a very confined quarters it could result in parunoia when it comes time for the bird to nest out doors.

Human imprinting, is over-rated if it does affect the birds in the wild it is because the chicks were introduced to a person or animal which they do not recognize as parents. This makes the birds overly trusting. It has been observed that when crows raised in captivity are released, they are apt to be killed by other crows, this is because crows have year round territorial; habits, and are very aggressive; the crow learns these habits from its parents, therefore a crow raised in captivity would not have this knowledge.

It may be posible to train birds to be agressive towad unatural or introduced competition such as the : kirtlands Warbler and the cowbird, Eastern bluebird and European House Sparrow, and Purple Martins to Starlings and House Sparrows. The birds would then teach there young this behavior. The birds would not be taught to be ugly; they will be taught not to be afraid of the introduced species, and that the inroduced species will retreat when confronted. Without this knowledge the species being tought would be afraid of being attact and equally afraid of harming the other bird.

IS U.S. FOREIGN POLICY PRO-DEMOCRACY

Even when the United States was a number of Colonies whites had greater freedom than anywhere else in the world. In order to keep from being totally isolated from the rest of the world, after having written a declaration of independence which indirectly called all other governments in-moral. Since all other governments were at least part authoritarian at that time; we created a non interference policy of indifference. Instead of being resented by kingdom's and dictatorships we were admired and respected; but not necessarily do to our foreign policy. Do to our in-difference toward other countries we failed to exercise our democratic rights in regard to foreign policy; as a result president's, and businessmen with foreign tie's using their authority without public scrutiny caused a great deal of damage to other countries. When it came time for revolution in Russia there was no contest between Marx simple idea and democracy; America had just moved into the industrial revolution with no antitrust laws, and unions were considered unacceptable, as a result many people were taken advantage of. Conditions in the United States were still much better than in capitalist Russia, but all the Russians knew was that the United States was another capitalism. In Russia then and in many countries today capitalism means the wealthy maintaining their wealth by maintaining poverty. Since the start of the first communist state, the United States presidents and corporations leaders have supported capitalist dictatorships on the hypocritical assumption that poor people would always choose communism over democracy. This support comes in all forms from publicly stating that they are our friends in one case we assassinated another country's leader. In order to

p. 72

stop promoting communism we must stop supporting authoritarianism.   There is no such thing as an underdeveloped nation; there are only impoverished nations made that way by injustice. Our own country has gone through many of these injustices but thanks to our progress democracy many of these injustices have been remedied. If we are going to promote democracy we must stop sending weapons and military advice to authoritarian governments, and start relaying our experience to these governments and to the people of these countries! Any propaganda by our country must then impartially show both points of view; in this way more can be learned from analyzing the incorrect point of view than can be learned from the correct view. It must also be shown that we do not have blind opposition toward communism, and that we disapprove of all authoritarianism. If we have made an improvement in the United States and that improvement does not exist in another country it becomes the moral responsibility of the United States to promote that improvement [it is about time we lived up to this big responsibility.
(NOTE RONALD REAGAN CHANGED U.S. FOREIGN POLICY IN 1987 DO TO THIS BOOK A POLICY THAT STARTED WITH EISENHOWER THOUGH HE BLAMED THE MILITARY).

PRESIDENT REAGAN'S NEW FEDERALISM

Newfederalism,   confederations,   libertarianism, conservatism; all names for capitalist anarchy» a philosophy created out of the emotional illness which causes people to take on the false role that to have any interest besides making money is irresponsible; and out of a paranoid fear of socialism, caused by these people's inability to tell the difference between regulations which interfere with free enterprise and regulations which control malicious behavior.

It has been falsely claimed that the Newfederalism is to transfer responsibilities To The States In Order To diminish the size of Government by eliminating Federal bureaucracy; the truth is they would have to create 50 bureaucracies of about the same size to do the same decision-making and bookkeeping as the Federal bureau's they are meant to replace the actual purpose of the Newfederalism is to decrease law enforcement and charity, it is hoped and predicted by the Reagan administration, that the states will not pick up where the Federal gov't left off. When red tape and inefficiency does appear, it is corrected more quickly in the United States than in any other country on the Earth. (note I told President Reagan My criticism of his policy would get the communists to read the publication and since I agree with it it is no trick I am always completely honest).

WHAT HAS BUSING DONE FOR US

Going to an integrated school not only eliminates racism in the student but also helps to eliminate prejudice in the parents. Prejudice is when the lack of knowledge of a subject, thing, or individual, helps lead to acquiring myths or fears. I grew up in the integrated schools of Norwalk, Connecticut. I am happy to say there is no one who was raised in Norwalk and is under 25 years old who is prejudice including those with prejudice parents. Busing is needed and will remain needed for some time to come.

p. 74

LEG TRAPS LEGAL TORTURE

No one can learn something they do not wish to learn.

Animals that are raised by man have greater intelligence than animals raised in the wild; this is because only man has a creative instinct. When a pet learns a trick he only learns that trick to pleases the owner. This is why the dolphin, who has a brain as complex as our own, will never be seen drawing a picture on the ocean floor, and why chimpanzees have been taught sign language and codes, yet they are not capable of creating their own language, even though it is just as easy to make up their language as it is to learn one. Most animals have less brain cells than men to do the same amount of work, slowing down the intake and sending of sensory messages. But these same animals think just as quickly as we do; this shortens their attention span causing a further limiting of intelligence. I have a deep respect for life; the respect I expect from other people. This petition is to renounce the leg trap as a goolish torture device, which is not part of the natural food chain.

The leg traps must be banned!

LIKE ALL MERCENARIES

In 1869 a fortune hunter brought gypsy moths to Massachusetts from France hoping to find a way of processing the silk in their egg cases; he was unsuccessful and he then allowed the months to escape into our environment. I first became interested in the problem of gypsy moth infestation when I learned that the Connecticut State agriculture department was trying to introduce a parasite [Brachumeria Lasus] which as far as anyone in the department of agriculture new could eliminate our native butterfly populations and severely or chronically affect many of our native moth populations. The department's claim that the parasite would mainly attack gypsy moths was a lie. The introduced gypsy moth is from France and the parasite is from Japan. I was told that this parasite was needed as an alternative to pesticides, and ' because the gypsy moth is an introduced species which has no natural enemies here; four of the gypsy moths natural enemies have already been successfully introduced years earlier, including a parasitic wasp [Ooencyrtus Kuwanai] was introduced which only attacks gypsy moth egg cases; it has been doing a good job of controlling gypsy moth populations ware insecticides were not sprayed. It has been agreed by all experts that an epidemic of moths can cause greater mortality to itself through starvation and the spread of Caterpillar virus; with only a small amount of damage as a result. But for this to occur no spraying of insecticide should be allowed.

The virus nuclear Polyhedrosis is being manufactured in order to be sprayed as an insecticide this virus infects all moths and butterflies just as insecticide would, but that is less effective and more important it will cause many caterpillars to get weakened doses turning their artificially contracted virus into a vaccine causing the gypsy moths to develop an immunity. p. 76

For those people who wish to protect the trees in their yards, Banding gives complete protection. Suburbs can be protected by using a strong spray of water from a hose to separate and remove the eggs from their silk casings, layer by layer; this causes them to dehydrate and allows algae to attack them. There will need to be a campaign to get each home owner to do the same since as soon as the gypsy moths hatch they make a silk parachute which allows the wind to take them a good distance from where they hatched. (note this was 1980 and most of the damage was a severe draught, and some people used oil on the tree bark which killed some trees I spoke to the leading scientist on Gypsy Moths Dr. Schwab at the Oatis Air Force Base department of agriculture Gypsy Moth Research Station for this article and to try to find support against introducing more parasites.) Apparently no one has heard the story of the king who wanted to get rid of mice. I was invited by the Department of Agriculture to speak to him on the day of the public hearing on the bugs introduction, I new it was a trick by organized crime to keep me from the hearing but I thought the endorsement of the Nobel Prize Nominee would work better to stop its introduction. When I told him what they had don that the hearing was that day the man cried and told me he was afraid to make a comment on the wasp introduction except to say the experts were endorsing a hands off approach for quick peek of population and the die off that would ensue).

JAMES WATT'S WAR

- Since James Watt took office as Secretary of the Interior he has:
- Stopped the listing of all new endangered species of wildlife.
- Supported efforts to drastically weaken the Clean Air Act.
- Dropped negotiations with Canada over a treaty which would protect migratory Caribou.
- Tried to halt acquisition of land for authorized units of National Park System.
- Announced his intent to allow oil and gas production on wildlife refuges and wilderness areas.
- Proposed curtailing the Coastal Zone Management Program.
- Abolished the Heritage conservation and Recreation Service.
- He made a public statement that he has instructed Dept. of the Interior employees not to waste time speaking to members of environmental organizations.

He considers converting all our forests into sterile tree farms an important goal.

High Yield Forests (tree farms) support no wild life. The trees are spaced so there is not enough light for undergrowth, where there is undergrowth it is killed with herbicides. The trees are kept healthy through selective breeding, pruning, and insecticides are used when necessary; this leaves no food or shelter for wild life. Birds avoid landing in tree farms because the uniform scenery confuses their sense of direction.

At the start of the 20th century there was almost no forests left on the east coast; people had witnessed the extinction of several common species of wild life in their own life time.   The public was understandably upset at the condition of their environment, therefore laws were past in order to regulate the exploitation of all lands, to purchase and set aside land for recreation and wild life parks, and to protect endangered species.   Tree farms were created in order to decrease the amount of land needed for lumbering, and replanting of trees became mandatory.   The tree farm was created so that we could preserve real forests; since tree farms yield a great deal more lumber.   Demand was also lowered by the higher prices, and increased use of bricks and steal.

Now lumber companies have been spending millions on advertising hoping to fool the public into believing that tree farms are forests which have wild life in them, and they are asking us to let them take over all our woods in order to make us "the wood basket of the world", this is James Watt's dream for the future or I should say nightmare. All of the laws I have mentioned are the responsibility of the department of the Interior.

Let your congress know that you do not want James Watt as your Secretary of the Interior.

(note after this book became a best seller James Watt was asked to resign and the timber industry stopped advertising there farms like they were wild life parks.)

WHAT IS NECESSARY FOR AMERICAN DEFENSE

We need to deter war; and Nuclear Weapons have deterred a third world war. We have enough Nuclear Weapons to over-kill twenty four times; therefore the claim that the Russians have an advantage because they have more warheads is the result of some politicians who have wounded egos because they feel we should have more of everything. The present administration and other politicians were under the misnomer that our Titan Missile Silos were vulnerable to a first strike; this issue was made into a launching platform for a campaign for a greater arms build-up. The main force of an explosion is created by the inertia of moving energy, most of the energy from an explosion moves toward less dense atmosphere therefore the impact of a nuclear blast is much greater above and around the sides of the blast. This is why if the Russian's strongest nuclear missiles are detonated outside of 2000 ft. from the Titan Silos they would not be damaged. Because we can assume the destination of the missiles are the Titan Silos it is a simple matter to detonate or even disarm those enemy missiles with short range guided missiles. Because the Reagon Administration learned that the silos are not vulnerable they have proposed basing the MX Missiles in Titan Silos. The white house has not announced the invulnerability of the Titan Silos since it would aid opposition to the MX Missiles.

In order to deter the use of chemical weapons the president should have made it clear to the soviet Union that if he again received evidence of further use of chemical warfare that we would produce and give away chemical weapons to the people who were attacked whether friends or enemies of the United States in order to deter the use of these weapons. Instead the president asked to stock pile

p 80

these weapons, in an attempt to imply to the Russians that some may find their way into their enemy's hands some day.

The Russian government has been telling their people that it is not Russia that would start a nuclear war but the United States might. This is why they did not manufacture the Neutron Bomb, and why they were upset when our president asked to have the Bomb, and why they were upset when our president asked to have the bomb manufactured. The purpose of using a Neutron Bomb is to leave potential spoils of war undamaged; the only strategic difference between a Hydrogen Bomb and the Neutron Bomb is that you would need to use more Neutron Bombs.

Most of our military hardware is not chemical weapon proof; we need to develop chemical proof equipment and filters, and we must mandate the chemical proofing of all Military vehicles.

It is currently being proposed that we install nuclear weapons in NATO Countries so that if Russia attacks one of these countries we won't have to counter attack in their behalf which is the way it is arranged presently; I of course consider this idea ridiculous since there is no target that we cannot hit in Russia from where we have the missiles positioned now. (note in personal letters I convinced President Reagan that the manufacture of any new bomb would psychologically cause others to do the same. I tried to stop the N bombs invention but my letter to the presidents military advisor was waylaid until after the government announced its invention I discussed this on TV and the government immediately announced it would not be manufactured. It was this publication which brought the soviet Union to an end with the help of Ronald Reagan who taught my advice and my cousin the Patriarch of constantinople Athanagoras who was head of all orthodox churches including the Russian Orthodox Church Christians in Russia were the persecuted Majority. and three anti

Communist organizations in exile in the U.S. who I contacted and convinced my book would have the same impact as that of Carl Marx.)

p. 82

Please you can see how important this is. Please read this letter on your TV Program.

I am writing to you to inform and rehabilitate the members of the Reticulum to Prevent Wife beating and worst crimes perpetrated by people who target Our criminal Justice system for their profession. The Dutch Meridian Church Came to this country in 1830 and named themselves the Ameridian Church. They told some of their member families **Not to have children**. They believe in reincarnation from your children. (I believe that all your cells go down the toilet at some time and we are nothing but memories and the spirit of God) Be that as it may, even if there is reincarnation it does not excuse Genocide. The Meridian Church had spies tell the **targeted people** that they could fool the Meridians by Joining their reticulum religion which they made up to trick them into not having children. They told them adopted children could reincarnate them. The Ameridian Church was successful in committing Genocide against these Dutch people. The reticulum still exists continued by Orphans of different nationalities than Dutch. They adopt Children without biological Parents and torture them into accepting their criminal beliefs without question. They believe they are sex offenders from outer space and beat their Wives every 12 days for having brought them to Earth Which they believe is hell. Their crimes include attempted Genocide, Spousal Abuse, Kidnapping, Extortion, Pedophilia, Theft of intellectual property, Bonded Marriages, and modern day Slavery, and I Arthur P. Vavoudis have been assaulted repeatedly Having been injected with illegal drugs which have given me short term memory damage. And they get away with it because they are Police Officers, Court Judges, Public Defenders, and District Attorneys. And FBI Officers who have told me they have taken bribes from the Reticulum. There doctors also steal and exchange embryos.

p 83

Please help me stop child molesting, wife beating, kidnappings, slavery, and overall meanness! By exposing the "Reticulum" as a cruel criminal hoax perpetrated by the Dutch Maridian Church. In the U.S. its called the Ameridian Church.

Where are your balls do you have any? I forgive you if you don't.

Every thing on the enclosed DVD is true. I believe it will shock people into changing.

I would like to spare the witnesses being attacked with Sodium Pentothal. They probably already have been; it causes selective amnesia.

You do not need a reason, to say you believe me! Just declare me Harry Potter. And everything on the DVD "The Autobiography of Mr. & Mrs. Harry Potter" ISBN 978-0-615-36664-7 as being true which it is!

Sample on youtube.com/watch?v=JT61GiRy588 or type "solutionjournal" into their search engine

Signed X *Arthur P, Vavoudis*

. Arthur P. Vavoudis AKA Harry Potter the biological father and legal Guardian of Joanne Kathleen (Rowling) Vavoudis. I placed her in the home of her surrogate parents to live I did not give up custody.
235R Main St. Unit 14,
East Windsor, CT. 06088- 9553
Phone (860) 254-5339

Email: vavoudis@att.net

Web page: http://www.solutionpublishing.mysite.com/index.html

p. 84

Velvet
the Crow

Arthur P. Vavoudis

Velvet the Crow: bird book and 3 Cds with 114 bird songs recreated by mimic bird watcher scientist and song writer Arthur P. Vavoudis   . at http://www. solutonpublishing.mysite.com/index.html buy by pay pall.

HOWARD DEAN, M.D.
Governor

State of Vermont
OFFICE OF THE GOVERNOR
Montpelier 05609

Tel.: (802) 828-3333
Fax: (802) 828-3339
TDD: (802) 828-3345

March 27. 2000

Dr. Arthur Plato Vavoudis
6 Upper Newton Street,
St. Albans, VT 05478-1557

Dear Dr. Vavoudis,

Thank you for your pamphlet regarding drug awareness. I appreciate your taking the time to write and share your work. Also, thank you for all of your efforts to teach children about the dangers of drugs. Drug prevention is a very important issue. I have forwarded your pamphlet to Jan Carney, Commissioner of the Department of Health, for her information.

Again, thank you for writing.

Sincerely,

Howard Dean, M.D.
Governor

HD/pv

Cc: Jan Carney, Commissioner
       Department of Health

p 86

"MIND SNATCHERS"

" THE DEVIL HAS A "
NAME !
IT IS

! SODIUM PENTITHOL!

About a child who risked everything

to save other children

A true autobiography by

Untied laces

Thank you for your kind words and your gift. The American people have given me the opportunity to lead our country in a new direction. I will depend on the diverse talents of every citizen to make the American dream a reality once again. I am grateful for your support.

Bill Clinton

Thank you for your thoughtful remembrance. I appreciate your kind expression of friendship. With my best wishes,

Ronald Reagan

Made in the USA
Middletown, DE
04 October 2022

11910664R00051